Poe
N

North Cheshire

Edited by Chris Hallam

Young Writers
First published in Great Britain in 2004 by:
Young Writers
Remus House
Coltsfoot Drive
Peterborough
PE2 9JX
Telephone: 01733 890066
Website: www.youngwriters.co.uk

SB ISBN 1 84460 356 3

Foreword

This year, the Young Writers' 'Poetry In Motion' competition proudly presents a showcase of the best poetic talent selected from over 40,000 up-and-coming writers nationwide.

Young Writers was established in 1991 to promote the reading and writing of poetry within schools and to the youth of today. Our books nurture and inspire confidence in the ability of young writers and provide a snapshot of poems written in schools and at home by budding poets of the future.

The thought effort, imagination and hard work put into each poem impressed us all and the task of selecting poems was a difficult but nevertheless enjoyable experience.

We hope you are as pleased as we are with the final selection and that you and your family continue to be entertained with *Poetry In Motion North Cheshire* for many years to come.

Contents

The Poems

The Dark

No light
No love
Only fighting
Only destruction

Dark
Damp
Caged
Enraged

Kill
Blood
Battered
Bruised

No light
No love
Only fighting
Only destruction.

Sean Kiely (12)

Hallowe'en

Everyone's frightened of Hallowe'en,
Because the witches come out and are seen.
The witches make a ghastly brew,
But they tell you it's a delicious stew!
So please don't come out on Hallowe'en,
Because if you are seen,
By the witches I mean,
You will eat their brew,
And become a *witch* too!

Elizabeth Ignatowicz (11)
Bramhall High School

Him

His eyes are hollow and lifeless as he looks deep inside,
To try and understand the workings of his mind,
He knows his heart is still residing in his chest
And once, long ago, it was bursting with bitterness.

He couldn't believe the treatment of fellow soldiers in the trench,
He couldn't believe the orders that were given, that were sent.
He couldn't comprehend the massacre of men left and right
And he couldn't cope with the emotions he felt and had to fight.

He felt the emotions dimming, fading like a flame
And now he sits wondering what happened to the pain.
The pain he used to feel when a bullet found his friend,
Or when he heard the screams from no-man's-land
And then slowly their anguished end.

His body still functions, his blood is still pumped by his heart
And yet he feels empty, alone and apart.
There is an empty heart residing in his chest
And his mind had been left to wander, to try and find some rest.
Rest from the images charging through his head,
Images of life being snatched abruptly,
Dying,
Dying,
Dead.

Jennifer Piotrowski (15)
Bramhall High School

Street Girl - Haiku

She sits by the street,
So still, vulnerable, exposed,
Passers-by stop, stare.

Helen O'Neill (11)
Bramhall High School

Seasons

Autumn
As the summer turns to autumn
And the leaves begin to fall
The trees change their colour
And the weather gets much duller!

Summer
Summer is a time for walking in lanes
It's also a time for fun and games!

Spring
Flowers growing in the sun,
Children always having fun!

Winter
Snowflakes fall upon the ground
When they land there's not a sound.
Children running to and fro
Throwing snowballs in the snow!

Amy Donegani (11)
Bramhall High School

Science

Tripod, goggles, heat-proof mat,
Bunsen burners, gas tap,
Safety flame then burning blue,
Boiling bubbles scorching you.

Solids, liquids, acids, gas,
Colours, smells, what a crash.
Safety rules fading in the blue,
This is science just for you.

Anna Goswami (11)
Bramhall High School

My Box

(Based on 'Magic Box' by Kit Wright)

I shall put in my box . . .
the winds of the world,
golden sand
the lushest green grass
and a fiery sun
to keep the world going round.

I shall put in my box . . .
a child's sweet smile
and a broken chain of suffering.
Animals and humans
will live in peace
to keep the world going round.

I shall put in my box . . .
a prayer for peace,
no fights or war,
no death or destruction,
no World War III
to keep the world going round.

My box is round
and hovers about
carrying my worldly possessions.
It's made of gold
and polished with brass,
yet weighs less than a feather.

Me and my box
shall travel the world,
helping those most needy.
We will share the harmony
and heal all pains,
keeping the world going round.

Ross Hamilton (11)
Bramhall High School

Another World

Stars twinkle up in space,
As glittery as can be,
They look like smiley faces,
Like happy bumblebees.

Jupiter, Saturn, Mercury and Mars,
Burning hot like the sun,
Nine big footballs glowing like the stars,
Believe me they weigh a ton!

The sun glows like a star,
The sun is yellow, orange and red,
The sun is fast like a car,
The sun hides, so we all go to bed.

Amy Belfield (11)
Bramhall High School

Love Is Like The Wind

Love is like the wind
because it is amazing.
Love is like the wind
because it is a craving.

Love is like the wind
because it makes you wary.
Love is like the wind
because it can be scary.

Most people say love is naff
but I know it will take me down the right path.

Natalie Gee (11)
Bramhall High School

Why?

When I crawl through the trenches
And look up at the blackened sky,
I wonder, why?

When I sit in my place
And watch bombs fly,
I wonder, why?

When I lie in my camp
And watch villages fry,
I wonder, why?

When I stand on guard
And watch mourning relatives cry,
I wonder, why?

When I run onto the battlefield
And prepare to die,
I wonder, why?

Catriona Livingstone (11)
Bramhall High School

Fires Fading

Fires fading deep within,
The hope which was is now so dim.
Like the day which turns to night,
It also goes from my sight.

Natalie Dunning (12)
Bramhall High School

Mars Bars

Mars bars are great,
Mars bars are grand,
but if you eat them too hot,
they will melt on your hand.

Mars bars give you energy
and keep you on your toes
and if you have a cold
you can stuff it up your nose.

Mars bars can be ice cream,
Mars bars can be cakes,
Mars bars can be chocolate
and they can be milkshakes.

Mars bars come in wrappings,
they are usually black,
getting them from our vending machine,
is really quite a knack.

Mars bars are neat,
Mars bars are cool,
but eating them in classrooms
is against the rules.

So what is a Mars bar?
Why it is so sweet?
Is it the chocolate or the caramel
That makes it taste complete?

Where do we find the Mars bar?
We find it in the shops.
Beware: don't eat too many,
or you'll end up with spots.

I really love the Mars bar,
I'm sure that you can see,
that without the humble Mars bar,
where would we be?

Felicity Howe (11)
Bramhall High School

The Sun

I am a ball of fire,
Sitting high in space,
I bring tans to your skin
And beads of sweat to your face.

Grey clouds are my enemies,
They bring lots of rain,
I'm always happy when they go,
So I can shine again.

When daylight turns to dusk,
I glow a pinky red,
So everyone on Earth will know,
It's time to go to bed.

Molly Greenwood (11)
Bramhall High School

Run From The Gun

Running, running, running,
that's how it all starts,
but the bullet itself is as quick as a dart.
Lying alone in a puddle of mud,
I think to myself, *how could I let this go on!*
We met them at the club
seemed nice at first like a friend would!
Stuff he gave me I didn't want to see,
as soon as I refused he wanted to hurt me.
So now I'm here wishing for a few more hours,
trying to get rid of the cowards.
My mind feels old, my heart's getting cold
and lonely I cry, when will I just *die!*

Lovetta Creese (11)
Bramhall High School

Life Through A Glass Eye

My dreams have flashed past,
my thoughts drifted away,
I have been sat here watching
and waiting all day.
I have seen birds soaring,
I have heard them sing,
I have heard church bells chiming
and imagined her ring.
The dreams I was having,
filled me with glee,
in them I saw weddings,
but the bride was me.
I saw streams and falls flowing
and danced on the grass,
I fed baby ducklings,
just so time would pass.
I swam in a fountain,
ate lunch in the park,
I watched for the sunset
and then it went dark.
But I had to awaken,
these dreams were not true,
I wish they were real
then I'd share them with you.
I'll just have to sit
in my wheelchair alone,
though surrounded by people,
this is not my home.

Evie West (11)
Bramhall High School

Cowboy Mayhem

They run around in their hats
but they are not toys.

They carry a rope,
they are cowboys.

Some films make you mad,
some films make you sad.

All films have the good
and the bad.

Cowboys make songs with choruses,
all cowboys ride on top of horses.

Cowboys like saying, 'Giddy-up.'
They fall off their horses, *whoops!*

They go around towns checking pubs,
sometimes they find odd clubs.

The odd bad boy starts the fight,
the cowboy sometimes goes out of sight.
Is that wrong? Is that right?

I bet the cowboy tells the cavalry
to take the bad boys out.
The bad boys shoot a victim, the victim shouts,

'Coward not cowboy,'
before he dies, before he stops.

The cowboy cries,
'Arrest me cops.'

That's the end,
that's our story.

No violence, no physical contact,
but can be a bit gory.

Adrian Cartridge (14)
Castle Hill High School

Cats

Sleep, eat and play
that is my day
I love to be loved and cuddled
I like to be kissed and snuggled
chasing bees and climbing trees
that is that because I am a cat.

Rachael Hallard (15)
Castle Hill High School

I Thought . . .

I thought the world was a small, caring place
Full of laughter and joy.
The screams of children's laughter
Dancing across my thoughts.
I thought wrong.
I thought the world was a huge, uncaring place
Full of evil and hatred.
The screams of children's pain
Echoing through my mind.
I thought wrong.
I thought the world was a huge, desolate place
Empty of thoughts and emotions.
The lack of empathy and creativity
Like closing your eyes in the dark.
I thought wrong.
I think the world is a small miracle unfolding
Full of life and new beginnings.
The universe ever stretching
Far beyond my imagination.
I think too much.

Jennifer Perry (14)
Penketh High School

She

The mother of all sins,
creeping up menacingly from the murky waters of Hell,
smothering her victims with her silky touch

She glides like an angel in a glow of green,
her radiant hair flowing wildly behind her,
smiling deceivingly as she hypnotises your mind

Unleashed she wanders the blackened night,
slowly entwining her death-cold body around you with no warning,
her claws digging cruelly into your flesh

She laughs high-pitched, manically,
tormenting your mind with her sweet voice,
there is no escape as she wraps possessively around you,
filling your senses

She has no mercy,
she pounces on her unsuspecting prey,
like a hungry wolf, desperate for fresh meat

She yearns to control you, infiltrate your heart and soul,
her pearly, piercing eyes trap you in their stunning beauty,
pulling you towards her in a wave of greed

She shatters love and leaves behind her a turbulent sea
of hate and destruction,
she will never stop, never rest, never sleep,
her thirst for envious blood is too strong

She is always hunting slyly for her victims,
prowling through the blinding mist as she lures them towards her,
she is ready to strike, she is jealousy.

Grace McNevin (14)
Penketh High School

Lust

I lie awake and think of him
Like a black hole he sucks me in
My heart pounds like a prisoner at my chest
As he sits down at his desk

He turns from his book
Laughing he looks
My heart is dying
What have I done?

Don't give up
Don't give in
My heart seems to yell
It's seeing Heaven yet it is in Hell

My soul stuck in limbo
Deep within my chest
Day after day an emotional test
Do I tell him or keep it to myself?
I can never decide which answer is best

Inside I'm crying in pain
Outside I'm smiling
Stuck in my heart is the pain and the suffering
Whilst on the outside is a girl laughing

Then it happened, he talked to me
All of a sudden it's like I could see
Inside I was bursting with joy
Now I could talk to this amazing boy

As he asks me if I'm free for Friday
I finally see
Just how hurtful,
Joyful lust can be.

Robyn Mannion (15)
Penketh High School

Alone

He stands alone, always alone,
Never wanted, never desired.
The brittle trees tower over him,
Waving in the bitter wind.
    He stands alone.
His cold, grey eyes are staring,
Searching for what cannot be found.
Longing for a friend,
Someone to stand by him, but now,
    He stands alone.
The screeching of birds echo in the silence,
He does not flinch, does not move,
Always searching for what is lost
And never to be found.
    He stands alone.
A crack of thunder, a flash of light,
The frozen rain begins to descend on him.
Though cold and wet, still he stays.
    He stands alone.
The brittle trees creak over him,
As though to comfort him,
But still he stays, motionless,
Never wanted, never desired.
    He stands alone.

Karin McClure (14)
Penketh High School

We Will Remember Him

Hopes of fighting and being a hero
Shattered in an instant,

The taste of victory at his fingertips
Suddenly snatched away

Feelings of fear and pride,
Honour and vulnerability
Ended with no warning

Where once a young man
Ready to fight for his country
Now a limp, lifeless body
Of scarred skin and bone

A cold, grey headstone
In a morbid but peaceful place
Is all that represents his sacrifice

A life snatched by the cold, icy hand
Of unjustified death

His name forgotten
His heroics not
His dreams unfulfilled
His youth still intact.

We will remember him.

Joanne Cocken (14)
Penketh High School

Depression

Standing alone in a crowd of hundreds,
Deafening silence pierces ears,
Darkness sweeps as the ground opens,
Ground opens, swallows whole,
An eternity of shadow,
Plague of endless night,
Tortured by a broken home,
With nowhere to turn
And nowhere to go.

Blood pouring from the heart,
Suffocated by thoughts forbidden,
Captivated by desires long dead,
Mistakes from the past to rediscover,
Voices screaming in all directions,
The future looks bleak,
No path to follow,
With nowhere to turn
And nowhere to go.

Joe Taylor (14)
Penketh High School

Autumn

A utumn is the start of time, when
U mbrellas start to fly
T his is when the wind begins to blow
U ntil a blanket of leaves covers like snow
M ay the conkers fall like spiky bombs
N ever walk under the trees!

Alex Grant (11)
Penketh High School

Revenge

There he stalks,
through the mist,
ready to envelop his next victim,
his icy fingers close around another's heart,
whispering mad thoughts to a troubled mind,
filling him with hate.

He drops in thoughts,
between heartbeats,
spreading confusion and indecision,
his eyes flare deep loathing,
the air charged with emotion,
you can even taste it.

An invader with this man's wife.
Unacceptable, whispers another thought.
Opening the drawer, blinded with betrayal,
he pulls out a gun and pants.

The trigger is pulled,
a man is dead,
the terrible hatred subsiding,
realisation sets in
and revenge leaves for new blood.

There he stalks,
through the mist,
ready to envelop his next victim,
after all, revenge is a dish best served cold.

Ian Kneale (14)
Penketh High School

The Miner

Out at last,
Away from his dreaded black pit,
The sun warming his dirty, dusty face
And his eyes light up with excitement.

The open field,
Surrounded by peaceful silence,
His long journey home awaiting,
Leading to his beautiful family he loved so much.

He stopped to take in the tremendous view,
So long since he had seen that joyful sunset,
Reflecting off the roof slates of the terraced cottages in his village.

The pain of being contained,
In that minute, claustrophobic space for so long,
This brought a tear to his eye.

He stretched to relieve his stressful pain,
Clicking every bone in his body,
But the tears didn't stop.
They weren't tears of pain.

They were tears of happiness,
For now he had freedom.

Callum Murphy (14)
Penketh High School

Alone

I had it all, one and all,
But I never saw,
Of the rules to the law.

I had it all, one and all,
My home, loans and family,
But now they are far away.
I had it all, one and all,
District with pride,
Jewels of all kind,
But it was just a crime.
I had it all, one and all.

Nothing is mine,
Not one single kind, distance
Is the key,
Far from life
And a family.

I have one thing, one to all,
A bed to sleep,
Myself to leap.
To give up and die,
Would be a crime,
So I am still one of a kind,
One and all.
No longer alone.

Christopher Sutherland (13)
Penketh High School

Peace

Peace is the sound of running water
Not running feet
Peace is the sound of children's laughter
Not children's screams

Peace looks like a delicate white dove
Not destruction and hate
Peace looks like a smile of love
Not wet faces from tears

Peace is the smell of summer and spring
Not of ashes and smoke
Peace is the smell of baking cakes
Not of fear and tension

Peace feels like soft white silk
Not pieces of an exploded bomb
Peace feels like a newborn lamb's fleece
Not of ripped clothes and blood

Peace tastes like melted chocolate
Not of the blood and tears shed
Peace tastes like freedom and hope
Not of confinement and loss.

Rosie Kerr (14)
Penketh High School

Boredom

The silence is waiting patiently,
Soon they will arrive,
The chair legs are starting to get cramp,
But this will soon go from the weight of their minds.

The waiting has now paid off
The kids arrive in line
One voice has broken the silence
But boredom now looms nearby.

Tick-tock the clock says repeatedly,
As they wait for the time to pass,
Nothing can really get worse
Than this same old boring class.

The kids are waiting anxiously,
Just a couple more ticks to go,
Ding, ding, ding, the bell screams,
As they laugh and squeeze out the door.

Sam Price (14)
Penketh High School

Bonfire Night

It's that time of the year,
Where the people all cheer.
There's a lot of *boom*, *bang* and blasting,
Because the fireworks are everlasting.
The sausages are sizzling
And the hotpot is simmering.
The bonfire is gleaming,
As the Catherine wheels go screaming.
All the fireworks are booming
And the rockets are zooming.
That man on the top squawks
And his name is Guy Fawkes.

Hayden Haughton (11)
Penketh High School

Being Me

If I had to choose
I would be myself
No one to pretend in front of
No one to put me down

If I had to choose
I would choose me
Someone I feel comfortable in front of
Someone I know will never leave

If I had to choose
I would choose my life
The life I enjoy
The paths I chose

If I had to choose
I would choose my family
The people who love me for me
The people who support my every step in life

If I could decide
I would want everyone to be equal
No one to feel small
No one to feel bad about themselves

So what would you choose if you had the chance?
Would you choose good
Or bad?
Would you choose kind
Or evil?
Would you choose your life
Or another's?
Whatever you choose be proud
Whatever you decide stick to it
Make sure you stand out from the crowd
Because no one should always fit.

Aimee Ward (14)
Penketh High School

Love

The burning in your chest,
the feeling of sheer emptiness
or utter completeness.
This is love.

No thought for yourself,
complete surrender of your soul.
This is love.

Like travelling through darkness,
with a candle shedding light
on the obstacles ahead.
This is love.

Breaking of your spirit
madness of your mind,
desolation, thoughts shattered
separation, emptiness, feeling incomplete,
when love is gone.

Sam Pennington (14)
Penketh High School

Christmas Laughter

Ice is forming
It's cold outside
Kids look in toy shops
With eager eyes.

The snow starts to fall
The trees are no longer green
The church bells chime
For the Christmas scene.

Daryl Viles (12)
Penketh High School

Indecision

As the black cloud of my emotions,
Hangs over my head like a lead weight,
Questions crawl through my mind,
Should I, shouldn't I?

As my salty tears,
Roll down my cheeks like a gushing stream,
Questions crawl through my mind,
Should I, shouldn't I?

As my beating heart,
Pounds like a steel drum inside my chest,
Questions roll aimlessly through my mind,
Should I, shouldn't I?

As my messed up head,
Spins like an ever-going waltzer,
The questions seep further away from reasoning,
Should I, shouldn't I?

As my breathing quickens,
Then slows down to almost a halt,
One question towers the rest,
Why have I done what I've done?

As my eyes slowly close
And the bottle of tablets tumbles aimlessly from my hand,
The questions are slurred and fading,
Should I or . . .

Katherine Humphreys (14)
Penketh High School

Love

Like a pot of gold looming deeply in your throat,
Sailing through your veins is the delicate gleaming love boat,
When you see the special person constantly shining in your head,
Weighing down your soul like a block of heavy lead,

You know when you're in love.

Gazing through the window into the starry, velvet sky,
The love from your heart reflecting deeply in your eye,
When you even try to think only then do you see,
For deep down inside that's with whom you want to be,

You know when you're in love.

Your speech goes all jittery in the presence of your treasure,
You know deep down that seeing them is pleasure,
Expressing your love deeply is all you want to do,
But you don't even know if they really love you.

You know when you're in love.

Try not to withhold it or be too secretively shy,
Because when it's true, your love you can't deny,
Let your soul lead the way don't hide it down below,
If you set if free it can only grow.

You know when you're in love.

Eddie Ralph (14)
Penketh High School

Justice

Standing before the judge
We knew she held a grudge
In her dark blue eyes I could see my fate
My mum and dad were in such a bad state
The sentence was passed
I hope it won't last
I'm out on bail until the specified date.

They say I'll get four years
Unless I get the all-clear
I feel as though my freedom is all but lost
I know that now only yourself you can trust
Betrayed in the frost
No one gives a toss
That soon I'll be locked away for years.

Accused of something I haven't done
There's no place for a good man under God's bright sun
I know I'm bound
For a life without sound
Because justice is not often found.

Craig Morris (14)
Penketh High School

Evil

I am the bride of death
The life that's lost in every breath

The dark between day and night
When shadows writhe in the dimming light

I am the piercing cold
Like zephyr through your trembling bones

The blood-red sun of dawn
Which stains the sky of anxious morn

I am your snake-like tongue
That spits on fools who do you wrong

The master of disguise
The careful tread of cunning lies

I am your darkest thought
With passion, power and pride enwrought

The heat of burning lust
The sensual thrill of fiery mistrust

I am both love and hate
Which squeals and shrieks at Heaven's gate

The source of all your fear:
The notion that I'm always here.

Samantha Kelsall (14)
Penketh High School

Broken

A part of me died when you went away
When you left me on my own
Just a half of a human now is all I see
When I look into the mirror
No thought for me left down here all alone
With the darkness in my soul

Who said you had the right to make me feel
Only emptiness in my heart?
Love disappeared with the wave of a wand
Making me an empty shell
It'll all be better once we're apart
Is that what your head said was right?

No voice comes to soothe me, in my solitude
No friendly ear to listen to my cry.
You were the one who kept me sane
Made me feel alive
But now this world has passed you by
All I have is the voice in my head

A part of me died when you went away
When you left me on my own
Just a half of a human now is all I see
When I look in the mirror
No thought for me left down here all alone
With the darkness in my soul.

Emma Pearson (15)
Penketh High School

Summer Lovin'

I see my angel walking past,
I feel my heart beating fast,
All the thoughts fly out of my mind,
A new feeling, a different kind.

Like the delicate petals of a rose,
An amazing new feeling I want to pose,
All my life I've wanted this,
Just like my first real kiss.

But that fooling didn't last long,
All these thoughts have to be wrong,
I sit in my world, all alone,
No one's here, I'm on my own.

The cold, lonely night leans in on me,
Each star twinkles telling its own story,
My life is over now that he's gone,
The air blows cold through the grass I sit on.

I lean back, look deep into the night,
I'll get through this, I'll hold on tight.

Faye Bellass (15)
Penketh High School

Kite

A kite is a spider's web,
All tangled and knotted.
It is a swift eagle,
Soaring through the clear sky.
It is a piece of lost litter,
Floating through the warm air.
It is an autumn leaf,
Snatched by the whirling wind.
It's a shame it doesn't know,
That if it soars any higher,
It will be swallowed
By the clouds.

Robyn Weldon (12)
Penketh High School

Emotion

I sit here in the darkness
writing as I cry
my heart is mixed with feelings
but my only thought is why

I can't get it in my head
why you gave me all this pain
you used to bring me laughter
now only tears remain

You told me that you loved me
you whispered such kind words
then you took off without reason
and left me with this hurt

I cannot get away from it
it's with me all the time
the imprints of your sun-kissed face
refuse to leave my mind

I bubble up with anger
every time they say your name
I hate you but I love you
was breaking my heart your game?

Laura Jervis (14)
Penketh High School

Hallowe'en Night

Gathered round the cauldron pot,
The smoke is rising, red and hot.
Cackling witches with pointed nails,
Bright, wicked eyes and creepy tales.

Werewolves prowling in the wood,
Their hands are stained with human blood.
Waiting for children, searching for light,
They'll soon be lost in an autumn night.

Pure white face and stone-cold eyes,
They try to befriend you with wondrous lies.
Vampires wander the night so dark,
And on your neck they'll leave their mark.

Dressed as a black cat with sparkling green eyes,
Hidden in the shadows until the sunrise.
Was it just me, or did the clock strike thirteen?
But then, after all, it is Hallowe'en.

Kim Bulmer (12)
Penketh High School

The Animal

This animal goes 'Woof,'
this animal is a beast,
this animal runs too much,
this animal creates drastic disasters,
this animal eats too much.
No, he's not a dog.
This animal jumps too high,
this animal goes 'Whoo,' at night,
this animal has no friends,
this animal is like a monkey,
this animal eats enormous eggs,
this animal is . . .
my brother!

Kaymen Ogden (11)
Penketh High School

The Modern Cinderella

Cindi was a lovely, sweet girl,
But she had a stepmum who'd make you hurl.
Her new mum brought two daughters called Charlene and Cher,
And all the boys said, 'What a right ugly pair.'

The sisters did nothing but sit on their bums
'Cindi clean the house,' ordered their mum!
She scrubbed and she dusted, she cooked and she cleaned,
It was 24/7 (at least that's how it seemed)

Cindi won tickets to the music awards,
'And we'll have them!' said the sisters (of course!)
To try and get fit they went to the gym
And when they saw Cindi they just rubbed it in,
'We're goin' to the awards and you're staying here!
There'll be loads of fit lads and plenty of beer!'

The sisters looked mingin' which made Cindi glad,
She didn't say a word in case they got mad.
The sisters took off leaving Cindi alone,
But Cindi got mad and picked up her phone.
She texted her best mate, who had a ticket to spare,
'I know that I shouldn't, but now I don't care.'

She got herself ready and jumped in a cab,
Her mate couldn't believe it, she looked really fab.
She got out the cab and walked through the door,
And Robbie looked over with his jaw on the floor.

He asked her to dance and bought her a drink,
He said she was gorgeous, her cheeks turned bright pink.
The sisters then saw her and started to hiss,
So Robbie leant over and gave her a kiss.

He proposed there and then, of course she said, 'Yes!'
And they live in a mansion just by Loch Ness!

Ashley Barrow (12)
Penketh High School

Bonfire Night

The air is cold,
The fire is hot,
Boom goes a firework,
That's a good shot.

Air is like an ice block,
Fire is like an oven,
Fireworks are like petals in the air,
Sparklers are like something you've never seen before.

Air is as cold as a freezer,
Fire is as hot as a radiator,
Fireworks are as beautiful as me,
Sparklers are as bright as the stars.

Cold, chilly, cool air,
Crackling, clicking killer fire,
Booming, bouncing, banging fireworks,
Sizzling, snapping sparklers.

Faye Savage (11)
Penketh High School

Bonfire Night

B onfire burns, brightly, blazingly, beautifully,
'O ooh, ahh,' say the children,
N oisy children watch the bonfire burn.
F abulous, flaring fireworks sparkle,
I n the night sky the moon shines brightly.
R ain plip-plops down,
'E rrr,' the people say as the food burns on the barbecue.

'N an, Mum, look at that Catherine wheel.'
I n stay the dogs and cats,
G uy Fawkes burns on the bonfire,
H appy children watch Guy burn,
T he night soon ends with a bang!

Louise Wilcock (11)
Penketh High School

Manchester

Manchester's the mantle,
heat waves of life,
time to turn into the fast lane,
the gateway to the heart.

Reveal the enduring symbols,
which resemble their ambitions.

Multitude of people
radiant across the landscape,
inspiration which'll last eternally.
There's no place brighter,
as their spirits are rejoiced,
like the uncluttered beauty of the past.

Inside occupies another community,
with their own square complex:
China Town.

Many guests have heard
the jewel,
Manchester United,
dominating and floating
at the top.
They don't play the Brazilian way,
but they play sexy.

Johnny Yip (12)
Penketh High School

Nothing

You walk along the street,
See families with nothing to eat,
No money, no food,
No drink, no clothes.

You walk along the street,
See children with bare feet,
No shoes, no socks,
No hair of locks.

You walk along the street,
You are not happy to greet,
No shelter, no base,
No home, no place.

Isabelle Howarth (14)
Penketh High School

Wilderspool

When I walk along to Wilderspool and all the fans pass by,
we sing along to all the songs as loud as we can,
I never thought I could sing that loud until this day began.
When I'm at the turnstiles they twist and twist around,
I give the woman all my money (I give her a happy smile).
When I get in to the match it is all very silent
I wonder what is going on and then the players run on.
I've never heard so much noise in all my happy life,
minute by minute, try by try the time starts to go on.
The atmosphere starts to end, the players score their last try,
just as the whistle gets blown, then all the fans of Warrington
just scream and shout so loud.

Today is the last match of the season
I don't want it to end,
but someday, somehow, it should all begin again.

Yasmin Gunns (12)
Penketh High School

Nothing

Nothing, I have nothing to hold in possession.
I have no family
I have no friends
Nothing good to eat
Nothing good to drink
Nothing good enough for my health
Nothing good to sleep in
I haven't got a warm bedroom like you have.
The only money I've got is taken by somebody else
What is left?
Nothing.
Go round to people for money
What was your reply
Was it, 'Nothing,'
What have you got?
A sleeping bag!
I've got nothing
In my backpack you can only find things
I found on the floor.
If the owner arrives
What am I meant to do?
I only have one choice
Which is return it!
These aren't my possessions
I can't say it's mine
What have I got in possession?
Absolutely *nothing.*

Hikmat Adebiyi (13)
Penketh High School

My Dogs

There is nothing better I like to do
Than play with my dogs, not one, but two.
They're up every morning at half-past eight,
To get the post which is never late.
It's breakfast time, their turn first,
To have lots of cornflakes until they burst.
Time for school, I gotta go,
Even though their big brown eyes say no.
It's half-past three, I'm home again,
My legs are scratched which is a pain.
Then I take them out for a walk,
They'd stay out all day, if they could talk.
It's time for their Caesar, their favourite meal,
They like it so much, you can hear them squeal.
Then I put them into their bed,
Where they snuggle down, head to head.

Emma Whitfield (12)
Penketh High School

Seasons

Spring is like a newborn baby
Starting a new life.

Summer is like a yellow flame,
Searing like a knife.

Autumn is like a beige rainbow,
Red, brown and gold.

Winter is like a bitter freezer,
That acts like it's old.

Ellanor Cade (11)
Penketh High School

Death

He is coming,
Creeping out from the shadowed corners.
I can feel him,
He is drowning me in his ice-cold breath.
He has snatched away the warmth
And stolen the sun,
Everything he touches turns to ice.
His long, thin, bony fingers reach out
Groping the air around him.
He has no eyes but he can still see.
He knows where I am,
He is crawling closer,
There is nowhere to run
And certainly no place to hide.
I can't hold on much longer.
He is the first bitter moments of winter,
The last dying seconds of summer,
He is the last leaf that falls in autumn,
The first splashes of rain in spring.
He is the cloud that hides the sun
And the wind that snatches away the flower of life.
He is the cold depths of the ocean
And the outer limits of the sky.
He is larger than life,
But he slowly slithers around unseen.
He is here, he is Death.

Frances McNevin (12)
Penketh High School

Homelessness

Cold and lonely on the streets
Searching for a loan or two
But haven't found anything to do
So I'm still cold and lonely on the streets

I had dreams once
Of all kinds
But now no dreams are mine
I sit on the streets and pass the time

Wishing and waiting for a miracle to happen
I've been waiting all my life
And now it's not even mine
I'm not even one of a kind

Where's my family?
Do they care?
Do they miss me?
Are they still there?

My feet are cold, they won't warm up
Colder than freezing
I wish I could sleep
In the cold winter's night.

Natasha Healiss (13)
Penketh High School

First Day At High School

Stomach churning, throat dry.
First day at high school has arrived.
How will I cope, who will I know?
First day at high school, I don't want to go.

Slowly, slowly I walk to school.
Bag feels empty, but it won't be like that soon.
Shoes are shiny, uniform is neat.
Walking through that gate is the hardest task to complete.

In the hall everyone meets,
Seeing friendly faces is such a relief.
All my fears rush away.
There is nothing to be scared of,
Life at high school will be great.

Lyndsey Sherratt (11)
Penketh High School

Snap, Crackle, Pop

Fireworks zipping, zapping the sky,
Boom, bang as they explode.
Sparkling sparklers twinkling like stars,
Snap, crackle, pop goes the bonfire.

Sizzling sausages burning on the barbecue,
Burgers hiding under buns,
Sticky toffee apples enjoyed by all,
Snap, crackle, pop goes the bonfire.

Oohs and aahs are heard in the amazed crowd,
Gloves, scarves and mittens are worn,
All wrapped up, nice and warm,
Snap, crack, pop goes the bonfire.

The big, bright bonfire heats away the cold,
The flames light the sky
Sending sparks way up high,
Snap, crackle, pop goes the bonfire.

Faye Duncan (11)
Penketh High School

Bonfire Night

Bonfire night is when you hear strange sounds,
Catherine wheels race, whizzing, fizzing around,
Big explosions from the rockets
In the whirling, freezing air,
Everybody in the crowd will just stand and stare.

The flames from the bonfire shoot in the sky,
Up and up, higher and higher,
Nearly reaching the telephone wire.
Bonfire Night is when you hear sizzles from the sausages
getting cooked,
Ha, ha, ha, from the children laughing.

Woof, woof, woof, from the dogs barking next door.
Miaow, miaow, from the cats inside.
Fizz, fizz, fizz, as the pop begins to get opened,
Safety is always handy,
So be aware, danger is there.

Jade Scott (11)
Penketh High School

Who Am I?

People often say
I'm a mammal that's grey
My ears are big or small
And I'm also rather tall
I have four big feet with extra large toenails
And if I'm weighed I'll probably break the scales.
I live in the wild
Where the weather's usually mild
I've got a very long trunk for a nose
Which makes me special I suppose
Yes indeed!
I'm an endangered species
I'm an elephant.

Luke Hickman (11)
Penketh High School

Bonfire

Bonfire burning brightly,
Sizzling sausages on the barbecue,
Children screaming and shouting,
Adults shouting, 'Oooh, aaahhh,'
And 'Wow.'

The sounds of the fireworks exploding in the sky,
The sounds of scared dogs and cats,
The crack and pop of Guy Fawkes getting thrown in the bonfire.

Suddenly the best firework of all goes off,
It was like the sun exploding,
But just then it started raining,
Getting heavier and heavier,
Until the mums, dads and children have had enough and gone home.

All that was left was Guy Fawkes burning on the bonfire
And the rain,
Until Guy Fawkes had gone
And the bonfire was gone
But the rain still drips on the floor.

Sophie Carr (11)
Penketh High School

Precious Is Time

the ticking hand is never still
no second spared for us to kill
minutes spark hours burn
race The Clock
when will we learn
our side, time is never on.
Rushing always, then
Tick Tock
dictates The Clock
another day another week another month
Gone.

Still,
their 'precious time'
wasted for nothing, except
they only sit staring,
half-heartedly hoping their hour might stretch.
But if my hour lasted longer,
just one minute longer,
I would wrap each second in tissue paper,
a gift
for You.

Eleanor Deacon (16)
Poynton High School

Golden Delight

Through the lonely fields I wander,
Alone as the breeze,
To seek the daffodils off yonder,
Sleeping under the willow trees.
No one is here but me,
I'm here alone, it's solitary.

I reach the golden daffodils.
Long live their beauty,
Reigning over the hills,
I can't help but be happy
At what is stood before me.

I cannot forget what's on this hill,
What stands before me now.
I feel excited, a rush of thrill,
Packed neatly in a crowd.
I cannot believe what I see,
I am so happy and full of glee.

Christopher Betton (11)
Poynton High School

Winter!

Winter is cold,
Winter is white,
Winter is coming! Winter is coming!

Winter, it numbs your fingers,
It is toe-curling cold.
Winter is coming! Winter is coming!

Winter freezes water into icicles,
Icicles so sharp they look like daggers.
Winter is near! Winter is near!

Winter is now, winter is here,
It's cold like the Arctic dew.
Winter is here! Winter is here!

James Bostock (11)
Poynton High School

The Key To A Child's Mind

The broad mind of a child
Could move a mountain and
The images of the mystical worlds
Could build the future's foundation.

The mind of a child
Could unlock the secrets of the past,
It could create a crystal of hope between nations
And keep trust between countries.

The mind of a child
Can relieve the stresses of life,
It could unlock what the world could promise,
And the world's sorrows could be washed away.

The mind of a child
Could discover the depths of the ocean.
And the sky is no limit for their imagination.

But the way to unlock this beautiful power
Is for no one to know, except the child,
Who has this great power, the power of great hope.

Sarah East (11)
Poynton High School

Cotton Bud Sheep

Cotton bud sheep are roaming the patchwork-like fields,
Eating tiny, microscopic blades of grass, they seem to move together,
Like a shoal of tiny fish.

A town sandwich lies many miles behind me, with large hills as bread,
And the town as the filling, with many different coloured objects
All moving around like sauces.

Children run around picking blackberries for a pie,
And eating more than they save, with dark red, stained fingers,
As their mothers chuckle, for they do so.

Thomas Seddon (13)
Sale Grammar School

Changes

Changes are happening everywhere,
Some people don't even care
That the world around us is slowly changing.

Trees and buildings being demolished,
Building apartments with a flourish,
Does no one care at all?

People changing from young to old,
People with warm hearts, people with cold,
Babies, children, adults and all,
Nobody cares, not even at all.

Countries and cities, villages and towns,
Some with monarchs wearing a crown.
However hard you try,
People will still cry, because they are unhappy.

Believe it or not, some very small things,
Like currency and money are changing.
From pounds to cents to francs and more,
All of them changing, can we take more?

So altogether the world and you
Are changing, evolving, what can you do?
By taking an interest in the environment,
The world will love you and you'll feel content.
However hard you try, people will still cry,
But if you love yourself and the world,
You're sure to get by.

Laura Jamieson (13)
Sale Grammar School

The Jump

Bungee jumping, on my way down,
The wind was blowing against my face.
On my way, all I could see
Were the dark green trees
Which looked like a leaf instead of a tree.
The snow down below looked like icing sugar,
It looked like Christmas.

I imagine the snow as vanilla ice cream,
All soft and creamy, awaiting my landing.
And as my parachute opened,
The breeze grew softer and more gentle,
And the jump was almost over.

And I landed on the floor,
I couldn't feel it anymore,
The sinking feeling I felt on the jump.

Jameson Lee (12)
Sale Grammar School

Looking Down

Standing nervously on the edge of a cliff,
Looking down to the beautiful countryside,
Filled with winding roads which look like wriggling snakes,
With cars as big as fruit flies
And fields like patches of grass,
I like to watch the people as they walk past.
Fields: green, yellow and brown,
Filled with white dots which represent
Sheep enclosed in gates.
Clouds hovering below, it's as if you could
Jump into them and flow.
I say to myself, this seems . . . like a dream.

Rachael Tither (12)
Sale Grammar School

Looking Down

Up above in a plane,
The cars are beetles, scurrying back and forth.

Up above in a plane,
The roads are long grey snakes, slinking up the country.

Up above in a plane,
The sheep are little clouds wandering across the world.

Up above in a plane,
The seas are large sinks filled with water.

Up above in a plane,
The trees look like broccoli on a plate.

Up above in a plane,
The people are ants going back and forth through the towns.

Up above in a plane,
The buildings look like pebbles on a beach.

Michael Jenkinson (12)
Sale Grammar School

My Place

My place is green, dark and mysterious.
The grass is a lush green, the soil as black as night.
The pond is a deep turquoise and a raven's shrill voice echoes
for evermore.

The flowers are enchanting, the indigo bluebells,
The blood-red roses and the golden sunflowers.

In my place you can hear the birds singing,
The pond rippling, the sound of traffic and
The wind brushing the leaves.
As far as I'm concerned, my place is magical
As the scent of flowers and lavender drifts through the garden air.

Samuel Wagstaff (11)
Sale Grammar School

The Glorious Garden

Sitting in the garden
With my brother, Lee,
Together we admire the environment
And talk about Dragonball Z.

The calming scent of the fresh summer air,
The sound of rustling leaves,
The succulent green grass on the ground
And the relaxing autumn breeze.

Dahlias, lilies, dandelions and lavender,
Mixed together in a world of colour.
When you close your eyes to relax,
It all gets duller.

The sweet sound of birds singing softly,
I could listen to them all day,
With the brilliant feel of the atmosphere,
Let's make this one happy day.

Tim McCormack (11)
Sale Grammar School

Looking Down

I'm looking down from the Eiffel Tower.
I see a greeny-yellow patch,
It's a football pitch that looks good enough to eat.

I'm looking down from the Eiffel Tower.
I see grey lines,
They are roads as straight as a ruler.

I'm looking down from the Eiffel Tower.
I see a glistening aqua strip,
It's the River Seine, as clear as pure water.

I'm looking down from the Eiffel Tower.
I see a multicoloured Lego site.
It's the wonderful city of Paris, showing off its natural colours.

Emily Rothwell (12)
Sale Grammar School

Perfect Picture

In Monte Carlo I was stood,
Looking down below.
The people looked like flocks of geese,
Gliding to and fro.

The water features, big and small,
Small cascades and streams,
Many fountains, small and tall,
A waterworld of dreams.

The luscious gardens, quite well sprung,
Many flowers bold and young.
A calming atmosphere created,
Makes me feel quite elated.

The animals like cyber pets,
Running through the water jets,
Many colours, shapes and sizes,
Having fun; no one realises.

Houses look like cardboard boxes,
Square gaps in the sides,
A wooden pyramid on top,
People walking in a lot.

A perfect picture in my mind,
Monte Carlo, warm and kind.
A picture I would want to keep,
But better rise before I sleep.

Holly Dewsnip (12)
Sale Grammar School

My Hot Air Balloon

In my hot air balloon,
I see long blue snakes curving round,
They are rivers.

In my hot air balloon,
I see small grey roots,
Ants scurrying across,
They are cars driving on a long, windy road.

In my hot air balloon,
I see large objects towering in the sky,
Filing cabinets scattered all over the place,
Skyscrapers in a nearby city.

In my hot air balloon,
I see cotton wool flying,
It is clouds.

In my hot air balloon,
I see a patchwork quilt,
It is fields in the distance.

In my hot air balloon,
I see millipedes going underground,
They are train tracks leading into a tunnel.

In my hot air balloon,
I am at peace with the world
And I have time to enjoy it.

Lee Horsefield (12)
Sale Grammar School

Looking Down

I was on top of the Empire State Building,
Looking at all the little brown and grey buildings.
The people were like little colourful blobs,
Forever moving around each other.

The bicycles were like little twigs
Being blown slowly across the floor.
The cars were like little
Lego bricks going opposite ways.

Everything was so small,
Like Micro Machines being flicked
Across the floor
By little children.

Little men standing outside their shops,
Trying to sell their goods to passers-by.
The buildings seemed to shrink at the sides
As they got closer to the ground.

Kristian Brennan (12)
Sale Grammar School

My Bedroom

The walls - a subtle shade of blue
Protecting me from my mum.

The floor - light brown,
Protecting me from my dad in the kitchen below.

The ceiling - bright white,
Protecting me from unwanted people dropping in on me.

The drawers - a soothing brown,
Protecting me from my dreaded homework.

The windows - grey and rain spattered,
Protecting me from the wind.

Tom Herring (12)
Sale Grammar School

The Blitz

Here I am, with a cup of tea,
No one in the house but me,
Peaceful, quiet, sitting down,
Then the dreaded sirens sound!

I quickly get up off my chair,
There's people running everywhere.
I hear the bombs, left, right and centre,
Quick! Get to the air raid shelter!

This air raid shelter's very small,
There's hardly room here for us all.
We hear the planes soar through the air,
The bombs are dropping, here and there.

Out we come, the noise has gone,
I think the Germans may have won.
Nothing but rubble on the ground,
Simple silence all around.

Sarah Medley (12)
Sale Grammar School

Christmas

The 25th of December
Is a very special day to remember,
Money to spend and presents to give,
Presents to give to your favourite relative.
Christmas cards are sent to school,
Whilst you're hoping not to receive one from a fool.
After your tea
And you have finished opening your presents happily,
And the day has come to an end,
You have no money left available to spend!

Natasha Fisher (11)
Sale Grammar School

War

Another day dawns with the screaming of the dying,
The endless shelling of 5.9s beats dread into our pounding,
terrified hearts,
Deafening detonations throw up clods of dirt all around us,
The hell bursts of the machine gun, flail men to death.
Bullet-ridden corpses fall to the ground, lifeless,
Suffocating men flounder about in the mud, like fish out of water.
The mud mouth swallows up the bodies strewn over the barbed wire,
The wind whispers the words of the Devil, corrupting their minds
and poisoning their thoughts.
As we walk through the decaying trench, stray bullets thud into
the walls,
A cluster of bullets decapitate the leaders of the column, throwing
us into confusion.
The death carriage rumbles past us, festooned with gurgling bodies,
Blood staining the ground where it passes.
How many more deaths will it take to satisfy the greedy monster
that is war?

Thomas Biddulph (12)
Sale Grammar School

Paradise

My island is warm,
The colours fade in my eyes,
I can relax now
As I am in paradise!

I look upon the magical colours,
They drift to and fro,
Like the bright green leaves
Upon the brown on the palm trees.
I bury myself in the golden sand!

I don't want to leave paradise,
I feel as though something is forcing me away,
But I will never leave *paradise!*

Katie Yates (11)
Sale Grammar School

Bonfire Night

The wind and rain were lashing us like a whip
As we shuffled towards the gate.
The empty, jet-black sky
Looked down at the impatient audience.
Suddenly, flames shot into the sky.
The dragon has woken.

Stretching out his fiery wings,
Reaching up to thirty, no forty feet,
People start to get frightened
As the dragon stalks its first victim;
Spitting with all its might, reaching out a fiery finger,
To snatch up its precious prey.
Suddenly, it had more energy, lighting up the jet-black sky.
People were amazed at its beautiful body.

Whoosh! Up it goes, a rocket,
Exploding into a fiery flower, the party was on.
Bang! A banger was lit, dancing with the jumping jacks.
A fabulous fountain cascaded over its pole, hailing the
ground with diamonds,
Children watched with an amazed twinkle in their eyes.
A disco performance lit up the sky
With ruby-red, sapphire-blue and emerald-green,
Coming from a disco light traffic light.
Catherine wheels whizzed round like boulders on a steep hill.
Boom! A rocket let out an enormous bang,
The disco had stopped!

The sky was jet-black yet again,
The dragon of fire dead in a coffin of ashes.
Crowds of people drifted towards the gates.
It was silent on the wet field.

Andrew Wilson (11)
Sale Grammar School

Why?

So many people suffer,
So many people die,
All because of war,
Can I ask you why?
Guns, hunger,
Bombs and greed,
These are forced upon
Those in need.
Wars have gone on
For far too long,
We need to stop now
As we're in the wrong.
Some children are left as orphans,
Some are dying of hunger,
What did Jesus die for?
Is he proud of us? I wonder.
So ask yourself are you for
Or against these dreadful wars?

Emily Tyrrell
Sale Grammar School

Scotland's Fields

Galashiels summer.
Lime-green fields spread with grey shreds of hay.
Sheep baaing, birds singing,
Peaceful smells of grass and nasty smells of horse manure,
The wind blowing past, my hair waving at it,
Rabbits running past and horses staring from far.
A beautiful view ahead of fields and hills.
Dandelions flying past.
The fresh smell of Scotland.

Jodie Collier (11)
Sale Grammar School

My Place

Red tulips,
Purple too,
All as sweet
As me and you.
Puffy clouds
Go floating by,
Soft winds blowing,
Like our breath
As the navy sea
Laps the shore.
The colour of the tree bark,
Brown and grey,
The sea as clear
As a summer's day.
As the children talk
Quiet and soft,
The wind moves slowly
Like a bird on a rock.
Behind all the noise,
My nana speaks,
Her voice as calm as the sea.
My mum's perfume
Floats about the scentless air
Like a butterfly in a jar.
The smell of salty water
Laps at my sense of smell.
The sun shines motionlessly
Onto the sandy beach.
The smell of flowers
Makes my hayfever worse.
The sun will set soon.

Chasey Slater (11)
Sale Grammar School

My Funky Room

My room has lots of colours, lime-green,
Bullet-silver sparkling and blood-red bleeding,
And the small spots of light
From my disco ball.

I hear my music playing, my TV starting,
Next-door's dog barking.
It's my mum talking to the cat again.
Yes, my cat is insane.
I hear in the distance the rush of the road
And my sister's muffled music.

I can smell all kinds of strange smells,
But the ones I can tell
Are my socks, my deodorant.
They both really pong.

Bubbly wallpaper and soft, fluffy carpets
Covering my room.
If you enter my tomb,
You have entered certain doom!

Peter Craven (12)
Sale Grammar School

Sodwana Bay

Green, beautiful, path brown,
Blue water, yellow sand!
Waves crashing, birds calling,
Leaves rustling, leaves crackling.
Bark lumpy, roads dry,
Water warm, diving often.
Sunrise beautiful, sunset better,
Sodwana Bay is littered never!

Gavin Dold (11)
Sale Grammar School

Bedroom Senses

Bright green, sparkly
Rhododendron-pink, pillows
Purple and white, desk
And wardrobe plain,
Pink curtains.

Television, cars, clock,
Mum, birds, leaves,
Radio burbling in the background,
The sound of the trees.

Carpet smell, seaside rock,
Warm, minty, fresh,
Slight smell of paint from ages ago,
The taste of my deodorant in the air.

Metallic, rough, wooden, sharp,
Cold things in my room.
Fluffy, soft, smooth, warm,
Comfy feeling in my room.

Cora Lynn Daffern (11)
Sale Grammar School

My Poem

I walk to the top of the roof
And stare into the far, far distance.
I look at the children playing,
Happily, happily, happily.
I look into my heart
To find that I am happy.
I smile and my heart gets bigger.

Sohaib Ahmad (11)
Sale Grammar School

My Place

Inside my place it's like a rainbow,
There's dreams, deep reds, Tango orange,
Pastel green, lilac, buttercup yellow.
At my place, I hear the airplanes flying low,
My cousin's voice bellowing, and her doll crying
Like a real baby that never shuts up.
With my eyes fixed on the TV, my sister
Imitates my running in, out, in, out,
In, out of the room.
The smell of fresh yellow roses drifts through the house,
And then the smell of food takes me to the fridge,
Like I'm in a trance.
The soft carpet that is laid all through the house
Makes you feel more than at home.
Be careful if you go to my place,
As you could end up lost.

Lucy Stockton (11)
Sale Grammar School

The Tiger

It sits around staring all day,
Waiting still to catch its prey.
When it strikes with its razor-sharp teeth,
It takes you down as if you were a thief.
Even with its orange and black stripes,
It's hard to see as there are different types.
This animal relies on its stealth,
Its reputation, as well as its health.
Even though it's just a cat,
It could still kill you and make you go splat.

James Kitchen (11)
Sale Grammar School

Where Is This Place?

I sit calmly in my room
Where the colour of the room is creamy-white.
However, downstairs, some people are chatting,
Loudly, not quietly.

I sit silently in my room
Where the walls are smooth and cold.
However, downstairs the walls are hot.
It is warm and nice.

I sit quietly in my room
Where it is silent.
However, downstairs someone is playing,
Running and stamping on the ground.

I sit in my room in bad temper,
I can't stand this noisy place.
I go downstairs and shout,
'How noisy can you get?'

I sit in my room again.
There is not a mouse squeak.
All of a sudden, there is
All the noise there was before.

Now I know this is my place,
Where it is noisy,
Where you just have to hear all the noise.
It is . . . my bedroom.

Victoria Hong (11)
Sale Grammar School

Where Am I?

Bright yellow, sparkling,
White flashing,
Red blinking,
Multicolours singing,
Down below, people shouting,
Horns beeping,
It's very annoying.

Can you guess where I am?

The metallic feel of the rail
Is as cold as *ice!*
The air is freezing from up high,
Looking down
From way up in the sky!

Can you guess where I am?

The smell of Chinese from China Town,
It won't make you frown.
The smell of pizza is like a slap in the face,
If you don't like it, then you have no taste.

Can you guess where I am?

Yes, you're right. The bulb above your head
Is alight!
It took you a while,
But now you can smile!

I'm in New York,
Looking from the Empire State.

James Hudson (11)
Sale Grammar School

My Secret Place

Sparkling silver, blinding building,
Against the gooey, greeny moss.
You can hear the people talking,
You can also hear them walking.
When the people flick and kick the sand,
The people also shatter all the shells.

When you walk onto the beach,
The sand is boiling hot and you shout, 'Eek!'
And when you run into the sea,
You make a loud noise and you shout, 'Yippee!'
When you come out of the sea,
All you see is a golden yellow.
When I turn back, all I see
Is the deep blue sea!

Richard Peters (11)
Sale Grammar School

My Family And Friends

My mum is really nice to me,
She washes, irons, and makes my tea.
My dad makes me laugh and feel great,
He's very much like my best mate.

My brother and I have fun together,
Even if there's very bad weather.
My grandad always brings me treats,
It's usually chocolate, or maybe sweets.

My best friend, Amanda, is really kind,
We play tricks on each other, but we don't mind.
My rabbit is so soft and cuddly,
When we got him we named him Flopsy.

There's one person left and that is me,
I'm a lively girl as you can see.
I have lots of friends and family too,
Maybe I could be friends with you!

Nicola Dragun (11)
Sale Grammar School

Sweet Shop

There's so much to choose from,
But which ones to pick?
Sherbet lemons or a tootie lolly stick?
It's the time of the month when I get my spends,
So I come to this sweet shop with all of my friends.

With five pounds in my pocket,
I leap with delight.
I could spend all day choosing,
Even into the night.

There's liquorice and jelly beans,
Fruit pastilles galore.
If you go into the store room
There's more and more.

From grannies to toddlers
They all come here,
The sweet piles get larger
Year after year.

I've made my choices, pockets full of sweets,
How bad life would be without special treats!
In less than a month I can go back once more
And gaze through the window of my favourite sweet store.

Sophie Mills (12)
Sale Grammar School

The World

T he greatest place in the universe,
H appy, cheerful, but now
E vil, full of hatred, anger, despair.

W icked people,
O blivious of the pain,
R egardless they carry on with their carefree lives,
L ost in their world while others
D ie of pain, disease and poverty.

Netesha Butt (12)
Sale Grammar School

Christmas

Christmas is here, Christmas is here,
Let's all give a festive cheer.

Children playing in the snow,
Little red noses all aglow.

Branches bending very low,
Heavy with the soft white snow.

To find some crumbs upon the ground,
Are little robins scratching round.

The streetlights shining through the snow,
There's lots of shopping, we'd better go.

Brightly wrapped presents under the tree,
Some for you and some for me.

From the church tower the bells are ringing,
And in the church the choir is singing.

Christmas dinner, tasty and hot,
Christmas pudding with a flame on top.

A lovely log fire to toast your toes,
To reflect on the day and have a doze.

Christmas is over, the day is done,
Didn't we all have lots of fun!

Victoria Keen (13)
Sale Grammar School

Pirates

Pirates, pirates, everywhere!
Don't look now or they'll give you a scare.
There's Long John Silver, his parrot too,
One-eyed Pete and the man with no hair.
They search for buried treasure across the Atlantic sea,
They never seem to find anything,
But they still search on forever.

Robbie Mackay (11)
Sale Grammar School

My Special Place - My Bedroom

Looking in my room
You can see
My blue bed,
With purple and pink covers.

I can see my pile of things.
Mum's been nagging me for ages
To tidy up.
My Woofy Westie teddy.

I can hear my parents talking downstairs
Which makes me feel safe,
My clock ticking.
Outside, cars roaring,
People talking, laughing.

I can smell my perfume,
I can feel . . .
My wonderfully white rug,
My bedcovers.
I feel underneath these and I pull,
And pull out Woofy Westie.
I cuddle him close
And I know . . . I'm home!

Siân Llewelyn (11)
Sale Grammar School

Night

As the wind whistles, shadows creep by,
The leaves rustle and I hear a silent cry.
I have an eerie feeling, a shiver down my spine,
It's like the trees are whispering, 'Tonight is mine.'

I look out of my window and see some bright lights,
I think and wonder what's happening out in the night.
As I close my curtains, the room becomes cold,
I curl up in bed and dream what the night holds.

Charlotte Birkmire (11)
Sale Grammar School

My Place

Emerald-green grass surrounding me,
If down a lane and up a hill I go,
I will see soft, sandy-yellow,
Crystal-blue,
Rippling water I will hear,
Horses going from trot to canter,
To gallop as they come near.
If back to the field of emerald-green I go,
I can change from fast to slow
As I encourage my pony on,
Back in the field I am now.
The fragrance of flowers greets me,
The green, green grass beneath me,
So I travel, travel on,
From trot to canter to gallop,
My horse's hooves going clippety-clop.
My friend is laughing behind me,
The sun is trying to blind me,
My pony's breathing is soft and quiet,
I can smell his warm, cuddly scent,
And the saddle is slippery beneath me,
As I gallop past a great oak tree
And slow down to canter, to trot, to walk,
And me and my friend, we laugh and talk,
I feel so happy.

Alex Fraser (11)
Sale Grammar School

My Place

As I stroke my dog, he quietly snoozes away.
In our cosy, calm place, the calming, subtle shades
Of the colours like the warm beach.
Red for the sun,
Green and blues for the clear sea in front,
Reflect the reds and the whites and blacks of
My medium-sized American cocker spaniel.
Objects surrounding me reassure me
To remind me that I am never alone.
Around my fragile body, the softly padded area,
With my pet dog softly sleeping, happily.

Where am I?

Michael Green (11)
Sale Grammar School

The Garden

Sitting in the garden,
Relaxing,
Enjoying myself,
Looking down at the luscious green grass
And the benches.
The great big oak tree is staring at me.
I sit in its shadow, looking at the sky,
Wishing that it will be blue soon.
I can hear the rustling of the leaves,
The barking of the dog in the distance,
The cars slowly driving past.
I can smell the conifers and the dew,
Clearing my nostrils.
I can taste the air of cooking,
The curry coming through the fan.
The garden makes me feel relaxed,
I come here if I feel tired.

David Meyer (12)
Sale Grammar School

Fish

The tail sweeps forwards and backwards,
Through the saltwater under the sea,
Dodging the corals and reefs,
Or anything that gets in its way.

The scales on its skin reflect light,
So it shimmers and lets all life see,
That it's heading up to the surface,
For air, and a midnight feed.

It returns back down to the seabed,
Its tail still creating the waves,
That ripple up behind it,
And disturb the flat surface above.

Then it finds a place to stay,
To take a break from its energetic life,
The fish will sleep through the night,
To prepare for another busy day.

Claire Ogden (13)
Sale Grammar School

My Place

My place is a hard, dark blue with peachy woodwork.
My place is where I do my homework.

My place is filled with smells of deodorant.
My place is a hideout when my mum's on a rant.

I can hear my radio playing.
Normally I can hear my TV going.

My place is cosy and warm.
My place is under my bed, on my dark blue floor.

Matthew Webb (11)
Sale Grammar School

My Place

My place is red and yellow,
All you can smell is grass,
My place is very big and large
And I can hear the commentators speaking,
The referees shouting,
The crowd cheering,
And the colours are flashing.

My place is . .
Man United.

Sophie Whittaker (11)
Sale Grammar School

Friends

Friends are funny, really.
Some of them love you,
Some of them love what you can do for them,
Some of them might even take advantage of you;
But they're still your friends.

Friends are frustrating, really.
They eat your food,
They live at your house as much as their own house,
They listen to your gossip and fill your head with their own;
But they're still your friends.

Friends are loyal, really.
They keep your secrets,
They tell you their most embarrassing moments,
they are here to love, adore and treasure you.

So these are your real friends,
My real friends,
Our real friends,
Real friends,
Friends.

Megan Price (13)
Sale Grammar School

The Witch's Spell

Hoof of horse, skin of snake
In the cauldron boil and bake.
Cats' eyeballs, bats' wings,
Poisoned entrails, gruesome things!

Simmering, bubbling, what a smell!
What can be in the witch's spell?

Dead dog's ear, squirrel's tail,
Scale of fish and fin of whale,
Eye of toad and snout of hog,
Rat's sharp claw and leg of frog.
Add there too some oil and lotion
For the ingredients of our potion.

Simmering, bubbling, what a smell!
What can be in the witch's spell?

Mix it up and stir it well
Sizzle and foam, it's looking swell.
Mould of pie and stench of skunk
Rotting apple, elephant's trunk.
Petal of flower, rose's thorn
Floating with a devil's horn.

Simmering, bubbling, what a smell!
What can be in the witch's spell?

The deafening noise of the witch's cackle
And the moaning of the half-dead jackal
All cooked up and ready to eat
Tonight we're in for a Hallowe'en treat!

Simmering, bubbling, what a smell!
Who . . . can be in the witch's spell?

Claire Curran (11)
Sale Grammar School

Damilola Taylor's Poem

You lived a life in which you were hurt,
A short, unhappy life,
A life of pain and harmful words,
All ended by a knife.

Your story tells a tale of games
That started off as fun,
That fun soon turned to torture and taunt,
The bullies' job was done.

You went to school one winter's day,
But little did you know
That would be the day you passed away.
It wasn't your time to go.

You live with God in Heaven now,
He made sure He welcomed you in,
You live on in our hearts, Damilola,
We remember your face with a grin!

Kerry Reid (13)
Sale Grammar School

Sleep

I close my eyes and I'm gone again,
Off in a world of my own.
As I look into the darkness,
I'm creating a world of fantasy.
Twirling, swirling, twisting round,
In my hole of darkness.
I'm looking round, walking through the cloud
As I start off on an exciting adventure,
I can hear a voice. I'm listening. What does it say?
I can't hear properly, but it's woken me up,
I'm pretending not to listen, but now I'm parted from my sleep,
Sleep, sleep, sleep, sleep. There I go again.
Zzzzzz . . .

Lizzy Philipson (11)
Sale Grammar School

If I Had A Time Machine

If I had a time machine
I'd see the sights,
Wonderful things for my delights
I'd go back to the past to fight in the war
And I'd go to the future to go behind the mysterious door.

If I had a time machine,
I'd travel the land
Or go to a concert of a famous 60's rock band.
The future looks bright, so I'd spend most of my time there,
Or go back in time when monarchs were fair.

If I had a time machine
I'd be so excited,
To make my friends absolutely delighted.
I'd be famous for my wonderful invention,
So I'd go back in time to the inventors' convention.

James Parker (11)
Sale Grammar School

Monday

I woke up on Monday morning,
I went downstairs and it was boring.
My mum took me to school in the car,
And I wanted to eat a chocolate bar.

I went to science and saw Mr Lord,
After science I was no longer bored.
At the end of the day
I wanted to play.

My friend was not in,
So I kicked the bin.
My dad got mad
And punched me on the chin.

That's what happened on Monday.

Daniel Burslam (11)
Sale Grammar School

Sunshine

The birds tweet, the flowers are fine
In the sunshine.
The grass sways, the ants get into a line
In the sunshine.
The children are playing, the clock chimes
In the sunshine.
And I never want to forget this time
In the sunshine.

Having a drink whose flavour is lime
In the sunshine.
We look at a tree, it looks good to climb
In the sunshine.
The bees are stealing, committing a crime
In the sunshine.
And I never want to forget this time
In the sunshine.

Making ice cubes, they will be mine
In the sunshine.
Heat is running up all of our spines
In the sunshine.
There isn't a bit of grot or grime
In the sunshine.
And I never want to forget this time
In the sunshine.

Helen Aylott (12)
Sale Grammar School

My First Time

Edging slowly towards the start
Butterflies nibbling on the nectar of my nerves
Called to the line; 20 seconds, 10 seconds, 4, 3, 2, 1, go!
My paddle dips the water as I power towards the first gate
Through it with no mishap

An immediate bow-rudder and I'm paddling upstream to Gate 2
I take the gate - no problem
Gates 3-8 pass in a whirl
My arms are pumping
Gate 9 looms like the onset of winter at the tail end of autumn
Dad's words of warning come back to me too late.
I take the gate too fast - my paddle brushes the nearside pole, *penalty!*

Through the mist of my concentration, I hear someone shouting,
'You're nearly there.'
My body's aching, my heart's pounding.
One last push and I'll be done
Every fibre of my body shouts, *'Stop!'*
Forcing myself to keep padding,
I race through the last gate and onto the finish line.

202 seconds for my first slalom - not bad!

Maeve Higham (11)
Sale Grammar School

The Sea

As the tide sways in and out
The seagulls soar in the breeze
As fishermen shout
Over the wind in the trees.
At night the sea roars
As it's calm down below
As the fisherman snores
And the ships start to go.
They are all mixed together
The ships and the weather.

Carys Templer (11)
Sale Grammar School

Broken Leg

A man sat on his doorstep
He was in a lot of pain,
His poor old leg was broken, it'll never be the same.

One day he'd seen a woman walking down the street,
Not at all the person this man would like to meet.
This woman was hard of hearing,
She mis-hears everything that's said,
And when he said, 'You look good in pink,'
All she heard was *'Your feet stink!'*
The next thing he knew he was hurtling fifty feet above the ground
And he found it quite surprising when his head went past the clouds,
As this sweet lady had punched him
Right off his feet and off the ground
And then he stopped,
In mid-air he lay, then fell back
At sixty miles per hour and quickly building speed,
Any second now and
Thump! Right next to his door
The sweet woman had left him.

And there he sat on his doorstep,
He was in a lot of pain,
His poor old leg was broken, it hadn't been the same . . .

Matthew Lyne (11)
Sale Grammar School

My Day Out To The Seaside

I went on a trip to the seaside,
On a lovely sunny day.
I ran on the beach with my sister
And collected shells on my way.

My dad and I swam in the sea,
And the seaweed swirled round our feet.
I quickly swam back to the sand
when we were about to eat.

We had yummy cheese sandwiches,
Some home-made orange juice,
Sausage rolls, crisps,
And a lovely chocolate mousse.

'Soon it will be time to go,'
Mum called at the end of the day.
'One last look at those little fish.
One last little play.'

I collected my shells,
And rubbed myself dry
Before putting my clothes on
And saying goodbye.

Kate Bennett (12)
Sale Grammar School

My Cat

A fur licker,
A mouse chaser,
A bird stalker,
A cheeky hider,
A face filler,
A snugly fur ball,
A lazy purrer,
That's what my cat was . . .

Sarah Robertson (11)
Sale Grammar School

My New House

I don't like my new house,
It has an earthy smell,
Dark rooms,
Damp walls,
A gritty bed.
It's very noisy when the crowds trample by,
I get no visitors,
No television,
No friendly neighbours.
My family left years ago.
All I can do is stare at the old, grey ceiling.
I would never usually be seen alive in this house,
But this is different, though,
I'm dead!

Peter Reynolds (11)
Sale Grammar School

The Fame Of Art

You might think that art is dull, but it has plenty of fame,
Once you do art - the fame will be obvious,
You may well be Gogh or Picasso,
Being recognised all around the world will bring you glory,
Not by being a celebrity, but by your talent,
Your fame of art,
Art is a skill - like football,
The skill of art is much better than any sport,
It's found in your brain,
It's found in your imagination,
It's in your hands how you manipulate this gift,
Of art skills.

Azhar Ghafoor (11)
Sale Grammar School

The Serpent

Twisting, turning, tilting traumatiser,
Twisting through the endless track,
Rattles the engine on the turn,
Leaving the engines on the burn.

Accelerating antelope
Accelerating to feel the breeze,
Cranking up to sense the whoop,
Faster and faster up the loop.

Speeding, shooting, scary, snaking serpent,
Speeding down the longest dips,
Up and up until the perch,
Down and down extreme lurch.

Whizzing, whipping, wilting wizard
Moving like a fast moving zip,
Pulled right up until the stop,
Then it looks just like a flop.

Flipping, fussing, flopping fury.

Elliott Oliver (11)
Sale Grammar School

Rainbow

Like an archway to a magical world,
Never-ending,
Red, the blood of a king,
Orange, a blazing sun,
Yellow, a summer daisy,
Green, freshly cut summer lawn,
Blue, the sea dazzling like diamonds,
Purple, tulips sweet smelling,
Pink, candyfloss, sugar and sweet
All the colours of the rainbow!

Sarah Hamlett (12)
Sale Grammar School

The Caves Upon The Orme

The Orme has many caves,
Full of mystery they be,
Mice run and scuttle inside the caves upon the Orme,
Go inside, have a look and come back out,
To adore the view from the caves upon the Orme,
Powered by the sun and the rocks that form the hollows,
Are the caves upon the Orme,
The Orme itself is large and beautiful,
As old as time,
Is the Orme.

The caves are lucky to have such a scape,
Passers-by are dazzled,
People who visit stare in wonder as the mining caves unfold,
Dark, misty and cold,
Llandudno below is unaware what beautiful sights are to behold,
In the caves upon the Orme,
The Orme itself is huge and full of awe,
A lump of glittering limestone,
Is the Orme.

Melissa Jones (12)
Sale Grammar School

Down I Look

Down I look,
the cars are the marching beetles on the pavement.

Down I look,
the ants scuttling around are in fact people walking.

Down I look,
everything I see - beetles, ants move around on the
grey snake that seems to go on forever.

Down I look
everything I see, my reality.

Atif Ali (12)
Sale Grammar School

Looking Down

I was high up in a plane.
I could see fields like a patchwork quilt.
All greens and browns.

Looking down
There were small blocks moving along a road
Some were green, some blue and reds.

Looking down
There were small Lego pieces which looked like houses
All red or black on top.

Looking down
A mountain stands tall and strong, shaped like an upturned
Ice cream cone.

Looking down
I saw sea washing up against rocks it was a
Sight to see, it disappeared like a mouse.

Robert Poole (13)
Sale Grammar School

Rumours Of The Dragon

The dragon is a powerful creature,
Myth or real no one knows.
Some say the person to slay one is a strong one,
Others say he is just a believer who can do as he believes.

Some say the dragon is one of many myths,
Like the phoenix, the leprechaun, the unicorn and the yeti.
The sword that slays a dragon,
Is as powerful as the creature itself.

The rumours are the dragon is beaten only by a saint,
Others say only a king or knight could destroy such a powerful beast
I pay no attention to such rumours, as even a common man
Could kill a creature of incredible power if he believes he can.

Jonathan Cobb (12)
Sale Grammar School

The Sea

The calm, soft tide,
Was gently rocking
In the wind
From side to side.

A storm is coming
Thick and fast
The calm waters
Becoming quicker and rougher.

The storm is upon us
It's strong and vicious
The waves rapidly
Crashing against the rocks.

The village folk are getting worried
They're starting to weep
Asking God for forgiveness
For the sins they have committed.

A boat is out at sea
It's all alone in the pit
It's frightening being on your own,
When your life is put at risk.

The storm is starting to clear now
The sun has come out
The rain has all but gone now
And the sea is calm once more.

Matthew Thomson (12)
Sale Grammar School

Dogs Are Forever

They say that dogs are man's best friend
And love to play all day,
But when it comes to being told,
They'll simply run away.

Now my dog's soft
And loves a pat,
But the thing that'll stir her,
Is the sight of a cat!

Now cats will go and do their thing
And birds will fly away,
But dogs are loyal and trusted friends
And love you more each day.

Next time you see a dog that's lost,
Without a friend in sight,
Just say hello and walk up slow,
I'm sure she'll never bite.

Now some dogs are fat
And some dogs are thin,
'Cause it all depends,
On the size of their din.

When it's time for their bed,
They'll say goodnight with a bark,
But early next morn,
They'll be up like a lark.

Matthew Davies (12)
Sale Grammar School

Autumn

Raindrops falling,
Leaves twirling,
Russet, amber, golden-brown.
Conkers falling off the trees,
Branches swaying in the breeze.
Orange pumpkins shining bright,
Witches cackling through the night.
Squirrels scurrying along the ground,
Looking for what nuts can be found.
Bang! Go the fireworks,
Crackle goes the fire.
But winter will come quick and fast,
So enjoy autumn while it lasts!

Ayesha Bansal (12)
Sale Grammar School

True Friends

T ogether forever.
R emember the first day you met?
U pset or sad they will cheer you up.
E very day they make you smile.

F riends are always there for you.
R emember your birthday every year.
I know who my true friends are.
E very day they make you smile.
N ever upset you.
D on't ever let your true friends go because,
S ome day you will regret it!

Katherine Alcock (13)
Sale Grammar School

It Doesn't Really Matter

It doesn't really matter, whatever you are
Black or white, boy or girl
It doesn't really matter.

It doesn't really matter, whatever you are
Tall or small, fat or thin
It doesn't really matter.

It doesn't really matter, whatever you are
Brainy or dumb, old or young
It doesn't really matter.

It doesn't really matter, whatever you are
English or Scottish, Irish or Welsh
It doesn't really matter.

It doesn't really matter

It doesn't really matter if you believe in God
It doesn't really matter if you wear glasses
It doesn't really matter, whatever you are
It doesn't really matter.

Amy Robinson (11)
Sale Grammar School

Instrument Of Fear

He's a Victorian headmaster
with a whip in one hand and an innocent child in another
Or a black cloud that keeps blowing and hailing, terrorising citizens
He's like a snake, coiled up ready to strike at any movement
He wears ripped trousers and a stained shirt
with the sole peeling off one of his shoes
His face so taut with anger could snap at any moment
with words of fury firing everywhere
His muscles are tensed up to take everything out on anyone
or anything
A fierce glare is branded on his fiery head.

William Robinson (11)
Sale Grammar School

The Special Occasion

Church bells are ringing
Church bells are ringing

A hot, sunny morning in May
Perfect day for a wedding
The bride has her hair dressed
Make-up and manicure too
Bouquets and button holes
Laughter and happiness fill the house

Church bells are ringing
Church bells are ringing

Now it's time for the bridesmaids and page boy to leave
It's very quiet now, everyone's gone
Time to reflect
Beep, beep! The limo breaks the silence
Too late for doubts.

Church bells are ringing
Church bells are ringing

Cameras are flashing
'Doesn't she look lovely,' can be heard from the crowd
Ushers are panicking, hurrying guests to the pews
The organ has started, the service begins
Vows are promised, rings are exchanged
Not a dry eye in sight!

Church bells are ringing
Church bells are ringing.

Tom Jolly (11)
Sale Grammar School

Tiger

I lie in the long, tall grass,
Warming myself in the sun,
I hear a twig snap -
It must be time for dinner.

I rise to my feet, head up
Seeking my dinner to be.
There it is, a deer
She's drinking from the river.

I edge along silently,
Careful not to make a sound.
Through the undergrowth,
My dinner's oblivious.

I breathe fast, my heart races,
Timing must be so perfect
As she lifts her head -
I rise and *I pounce!*

I stand tall, proud and stripy.
Satisfied with my killing,
My dinner is all eaten
I am the tiger!

Natalie Barnes (11)
Sale Grammar School

Trains!

T rains are fast, trains are slow,
R ide them ten days in a row,
A lso trains are very long,
I f you're on one have a little sing-song,
N o one dislikes trains,
S o why don't you go on one when it rains.

Scott Brown (11)
Sale Grammar School

The Big Race

It is the night before the big race
And everyone is sound.
I lay here wide awake,
Wondering how I will do.

What if I come first?
What if I come last?
What if I do well?
What if I do bad?

It is the morning of the big race
And everyone is awake,
I am still sleepy,
From being awake last night.

My heart thumps my chest hard,
I think it will break out.
My throat is dry and my hands are cold
And the winter's cold is hitting my legs.

Three words then hit me,
Ready, set and go.
I look around and everyone runs,
I think I may too.

It is the middle of the race
And I am coming first.
My legs are aching a bit,
But I'll be OK.

It is near the end of the race
And I am still coming first.
I can hear the screams from spectators,
As I whizz around the bend.

Just a couple more yards to go,
Must keep running.
Nearly there, nearly there
And . . .

It is the end of the race,
I came last.
I fell flat on my face,
I shall never run a race again.

Aimée Garner (11)
Sale Grammar School

The Creepy Wood

The wood is full of creepy trees,
The wood is full of whispering breeze,
The wood is full of scary sights,
It's dangerous to go into the wood at night.

I met a man with three eyes on each hand
And a body covered with watery sand,
He had a tree sticking out of his head
And a backwards poem he creepily read.

The man cast a spell on me
And invited me to a witches' tea.
He turned me into a slimy frog
And put me in a room with a hog.

The hog was really scary too,
Not like one found in a zoo,
Out of his belly came a beam,
Oh! Phew! It was just a scary dream.

I suddenly woke up shining with sweat
And thought about my nightmare with shivering dread.
Later, I laughed at myself for believing such a thing
And went to bed after having a cold, refreshing drink.

Sundus Zafar (12)
Sale Grammar School

My Family And My Fish

M y family and my fish are very different
Y ou'd be surprised by the amounts I've had.

F irst of all there's my dad, he's worked in loads of places
A nd he loves tidying up
M um is next, she plays netball and teaches
I think I get my brains from her
L ike me, my brother is at SGS
Y ou know the only thing is he's done so much I can't keep up.

A fter my family you'd think it would be my friends but . . .
N ot another poem about friends you'd say, so . . .
D ifferent that's me, I'm writing about my fish.

M y first fish was Star, all shimmering and bright
Y ou know she was my favourite, I cried when she died.

F ish are cool, you know so,
I had Speedy and Star second, in-between
S o now I've got Star the third and unfortunately . . .
H ey, that's the end so now you know about my . . .
family and my fish.

Grace Ogden (11)
Sale Grammar School

Fireworks

F izz, whoosh goes the luminous waterfall.
I nto the night sky fire the rockets.
R ed, green and blue sparks all around.
E very corner brightly lit.
W onderstruck faces watch with awe.
O range and yellow flames flickering before you.
R ound and round whizz the Catherine wheels.
K eeping you warm is the bright, burning bonfire.
S oon as it had all started . . . it stopped.

Lucy Gorman (11)
Sale Grammar School

The Witches!

The witches mumble horrid chants,
You're scalded by five thousand ants,
A Martian pulls a fearsome face
And throws you into outer space
You're tied in front of whistling trains,
A tomahawk has sliced your brains,
The tigers snarl, the giants roar,
You're sat on by a dinosaur
In vain you're shouting, 'Help,' and 'Stop,'
The walls are spinning like a top
The Earth is melting in the sun
And all the horror's just begun.
And oh the screams, the thumping hearts
That unthinkable night before school starts.

Douglas Whyley (11)
Sale Grammar School

Looking Down

As the gentle wind pushes,
We travel further west,
I can see the countryside way down below,
As I look out from the basket of our hot air balloon.

When I look down on the fields I see an organic patchwork blanket
And the river, a brown winding worm.
The roads, a thin pencil line and the cars are like Lego bricks
zooming along.

As we rise higher and higher, the people are now smaller than ants
And the villages are piles of rock, cemented together by a bricklayer.
The trees become green cotton wool balls
As I look further out I can see the suburbs of a large city
forming on the horizon.

Elizabeth Dunn (12)
Sale Grammar School

Looking Down

As the plane glides through the air,
I look out of my window and see,
Roads curving and twisting like a snake,
All these things look so small to me.

The plants look like coloured dots,
The river is long and gleaming blue,
The little people I can hardly see
And the trees and bushes are like green blobs too.

It all looks like a watercolour painting,
Painted all precise and neat,
The buildings like dark, shadowed shapes
And the cars are as small as grains of wheat.

Leanne Feeney (12)
Sale Grammar School

The Seasons

A field of daffodils swaying gold,
The sun glowing warm,
A fresh, gentle breeze blowing,
Field mice poking their tiny heads up in search of light.

Children run out of school excited about the summer holidays,
Jumping in paddling pools, having fun,
Laughing and playing outside,
Getting on planes, going abroad!

Collecting conkers and having fights,
Falling leaves; yellow, orange, brown
Squirrels collecting nuts for the winter
Misty and foggy.

Cold, wet and snowy,
Children wrapping up in scarves and gloves,
Snowmen being made,
Christmas trees being put up and decorated.

Rachel Colwell (11)
Sale Grammar School

Opposites!

Summer and winter
Summer and winter are different dates,
Summer is a sunny day.
Winter is a snowy day.
Summer is a day outside.
Winter is a day inside.
Summer is a serve at tennis.
Winter is a scrum at rugby.

Heaven and Hell
Heaven and Hell are different places,
Heaven is a calming place.
Hell is a radical place.
Heaven is a quiet estate.
Hell is an industrial estate.

Me and my sister
Me and my sister are a match of goodwill,
I am a playful boy.
My sister is a playful girl.
I am a kind boy,
I'll buy my sister an exciting toy.
My sister is a kind girl,
She'll let me have a lick of her ice swirl.
Me and my sister are not like the rest
We are not opposite, we are the same!

Robert Hudson (11)
Sale Grammar School

I Never Can

I never can, I never will
See I've got a dream I can't fulfil
The thing is my friend I cannot rhyme
But I better do in the nick of time.

For my English teacher wants me to
Write a poem before half-past two
And never before in my life
Have I had to make this sacrifice.

A lunchtime play is just too much
I can't even smell or touch
The fresh air that is always clean
And the beautiful grass that's always green.

Here I am at 29 past 2
I wasted my time writing to you
Another F won't get me far
But, 'What Miss, I got an A Star!'

Michael Norton (11)
Sale Grammar School

The World

The world is a big place,
Located somewhere in space.

There are lots of wars going on,
Lives are wasted, lives are gone.

Babies are born,
As lives are torn.

People fighting for what they believe in,
Lives will be lost, but who will win?

Hopefully one day all the war will cease
And throughout the world there will be peace.

Sophie Black (11)
Sale Grammar School

On Top Of A Very, Very High Tree

On top of a very, very high tree,
Many people are what I can see.
People who look like coloured stick men
And people who are an ink blob off a pen.

Down on the floor there is a deer
And a fire engine is what I can hear.
I look to my left and I see a big blob,
Its flashing lights show it is on a job.

It sticks out from the rest
And seems to be heading towards the west.
I can see a long, winding blue line,
it is the river, called the River of Nine.

It is getting colder up here in this tree,
The wind sways this tree that is what I can see.
The ground moves and I grip harder against the trunk,
There are great big pieces of rock on the floor which look like
small little chunks.

I can hear the fire trucks coming near
And I can hear my name being called up here.
I look down and see a small fireman,
He is climbing a ladder towards me that is their plan.

I can see his features now he is up high,
He is very shaky and scared, but so am I.
'Do you trust me?' he screams and shouts,
I say, 'Yes,' but I still have my doubts.

As we climb down the long, creaky ladder towards my
family and friends,
It feels weird as my long, terrifying adventure finally ends.
As I walk along on the ground which is as safe as it can be,
I suddenly feel that I wish I was still up in that big tree.

Lydia Gaunt (12)
Sale Grammar School

War And Peace

War is like a thundering tornado,
destroying everything in its path,
a fiery dragon, a bloodied corpse,
choking, killing, polluting fumes,
that's what war is . . .

Peace is like lying on a sun-kissed beach,
pure, total, heavenly serenity,
a cuddly teddy, a healthy child,
happiness, loving everywhere,
that's what peace is . . .

War is hate, peace is caring,
Peace is strong, but war is brutal,
loved ones lie dead in their graves,
or painfully dying in a foreign land,
Peace is none of these, but more like trees and foliage,
people die for their country,
but war is never won . . .

Peace is like a fluffy cloud,
War is like boiling lava,
Which would you prefer?

Sam Moorhouse (12)
Sale Grammar School

Sharks

They come in many different types,
Tiger, Thrasher, and great white,
They all have a deadly bite,
You hear a scream break the silence of the night.

In water cold, shallow or deep,
A shark that swims will never sleep,
You see the fin, you start to scream,
The jaws bite you in half, clean.

A passer-by will hear your cries,
Alerts the police before the person dies,
The police arrive, are they too late?
Yes, the person was like a shark's bait.

But now the police could kill the shark,
With harpoon gun and deadly dart,
The puff of darts, the sound of guns,
All the fathers and their sons.

Finally a bullet pierced its head,
With a loud cry, the shark dropped dead,
The body was hung up for all to see,
Just what a terror, a shark can be.

Daniel Corker (12)
Sale Grammar School

A Poem About Field Lacrosse

F ield lacrosse is a sport
I nteresting
E xciting
L acrosse is a fierce and fast game
D efence tactics are often used

L eft and right hand dodges fast
A ttack tactics all the time
C hecking is used in attack, defence and midfield crash, smack
R otating around the opponent so fast
O ver the field to get to the goal
S ight of the game is fierce and swift
S wift as a cheetah the players run
E ndurance is needed to win the game.

Alexander Oliver (11)
Sale Grammar School

Summer

School's out!
It's summertime,
Time to play in the park,
Time to splash in the water,
The sun is shining down on me,
Keep in the shade!
I know I'll burn,
(I don't take good to the sun!)
Put on suncream,
Now I'm safe!
I jump in the pool
And land with a *splash!*
I've had fun today
But now I must rest,
I'll see you tomorrow,
When we'll be playing in the park.

Kyle Fallon (11)
Sale Grammar School

The Sea

The sea is a calming cat,
Its waves gently coming in.
The sea now is gentle
Waiting for children to begin bathing.

Boys, girls, men, women,
Run swiftly and dive into the sea,
The sea now has got its chance
It knows what to be.

The sea transforms into a crafty crocodile!

The sea is a crafty crocodile,
He has caught his prey, the children struggling.
The crocodile's mouth swallowing the children,
Sending them to their death.

At night the sea is at the peak,
Smashing through the sand.
Its waves go over the wave breakers,
Even over Scarborough beach's wall.

However, when summer comes,
The sun drives the crocodile back.
The loyal lion protects the waters,
The crocodile not daring to return however.

The crocodile however plans his revenge to hit back in the winter.

Thomas Powell (11)
Sale Grammar School

The Great War

The canons went *bang!*
The guns went *boom!*
The war had started and it was half-past noon.

The planes flew over up ahead
Dropped their bombs
And the Germans were dead.

Here come the troops, sailing in
Bullets were flying
And one hit my chin.

Down and down the medics took me
Deep underground
And then they searched me.

Back on the battlefield I went
Only to get captured by some
Nazi men.

So there I sat waiting to die
But instantly they shot me
In the eye.

The canons went *bang!*
The guns went boom!
The war was over and the troops will be home soon.

Oliver Janes (12)
Sale Grammar School

Looking Down

I'm jumping off a cliff
And can see everything below me.
I see hundreds of trees,
They look like little peas.

I'm jumping off a cliff
The rivers look like streams.
The bridges look like metal beams,
The lake looks like a baby's bath.

I'm jumping off a cliff
The motorways look like paths
The cars look like little toys
The pylons look like baby boys.

I'm jumping off a cliff
The elephants look like grey stones
The warehouses look like mobile phones
With lorries as the antennae.

Lanza Krusen
Sale Grammar School

Moving House

An immense truck pulled into our drive,
Just how long will it be until we arrive?
Our new house awaits, all fresh and clean,
Ready and waiting fit for a queen.

As we opened the great creaking door,
And walked across the golden tiled floor,
We are in our new house, here to stay.
Here together, to work, rest and play.

We trudged in with our cases,
Like tramps off the street,
Not long to go
Until we put up our feet!

Matthew Volp (11)
Sale Grammar School

When I Went On Holiday

When I went on holiday,
I had a great time,
When I went on holiday,
I heard an Irish rhyme.

When I went on holiday,
I ate some foreign food,
When I went on holiday,
I was in a good mood.

When I went on holiday,
I had a lot of money,
When I went on holiday,
I bought a jar of honey.

When I went on holiday,
I saw a bird fly,
When I went on holiday,
I had to say bye-bye.

James Fletcher (12)
Sale Grammar School

Chocolate

Chocolate is white and brown
Chocolate wears a golden crown
Chocolate's nice
Chocolates taste creamy
Chocolate makes me dreamy
Chocolate comes in many forms
You can drink chocolate
It is not very healthy
But I don't care
Chocolate's there when you're
Stressed, depressed, lonely and hurt
Chocolate is there for everyone
Except my dad who is diabetic.

Daniel Stone (11)
Sale Grammar School

The Leaf

Gently floating in the breeze
Attached to a twig with other leaves,
Down below a babbling brook,
Up above, the icy sun shining through the tree,
I break away and flutter down
Into the jaws of the icy water,
I flutter in and am washed away with several other leaves,
The icy moor way downstream looms in front of me.

I catch on rocks and twigs and roots in the icy water
Until I reach the moor, dark and forbidding,
The brook trickles through the brambles overgrowing into the water
Brambles hold me fast,
Other leaves bump into me and they are also snared.
Flood waters hit us and we are swooshed away,
Even though this helps me
I am merely a skeleton,
Fading back to where I came.

Charles Learmont (12)
Sale Grammar School

Sadie

Sadie my dog is as black as coal,
Sadie my dog likes to dig a hole.

Sadie my dog when jumping for balls,
Sadie my dog never comes when called.

Sadie my dog has a big, wet nose,
Sadie my dog is washed with a hose.

Sadie my dog has a waggy tail,
Sadie my dog tries to eat the mail.

Sadie my dog has a very loud bark, but
Sadie my dog most likes a walk in the park.

Emma Bagshaw (11)
Sale Grammar School

Man's Best Friend

M an's best friend is of course the brave, friendly dog.
A lways there, always cares, growling at strangers like a grizzly bear.
N ever cowardly running away, never being friendly to those they don't know.
S ome dogs don't understand the above rules and like mine are completely bonkers.

B onkers should be her name as bonkers is definitely her game.
E ager my dog is just that, eager for biscuits a treat and a pat.
S caredness she has that too, when the Hoover comes out, there's hullabaloo.
T ug of war, her favourite game of course, chewies, ropes, even slippers, my dog's used them all.

F ood, my dog really loves food the best thing in the world.
R hubarb the only food my dog hates.
I ndividual, she is just that, a true Dalmatian to the end.
E veryone wants to give her a pat, but my dog really doesn't mind that.
N ever naughty, never bad, always happy, always glad.
D og is man's best friend and will stay that way until the end.

Rebecca Bennett (12)
Sale Grammar School

Autumn

The wind whispered through the trees,
The sky was like a wave of clouds,
The rustling leaves
In the calm, gentle breeze.

The rain trickled like a waterfall of mist,
The moon was a lone light drifting in the night sky,
The stars glinted, like a dark abyss of diamonds
And the small birds and animals, like an army of night creatures,
Staring like an owl, hunting for its prey.

Jack Bain (11)
Sale Grammar School

The Teacher From Sale

There once was a teacher from Sale
She was stuck in a very bad gale.
The wind blew her over,
And her dog Rover,
And they both ended up in Hale.
They carried on with their journey,
When they came to a shop selling chutney,
They went inside,
But it wasn't wide,
So they continued their journey on donkey.
The donkey was getting tired,
So another one they hired,
This donkey was small,
It wasn't good at all,
So he they quickly fired.
They didn't know what to do,
Until they thought of something new.
They went on a plane,
Which took them to Spain,
And there the sky was blue.
Eventually Spain got boring,
The rain started pouring,
They flew back down,
To Sale, their home town,
But the school work was appalling.
But she realised her life wasn't bad,
And she stopped being so sad.
She bought a new house,
A cat and a mouse,
And even the dog was glad!

Rosie Peters (11)
Sale Grammar School

Sweet 'N' Sour Rap

Chocolate, Haribo, Dairy Milks
These are sweet things that I love
Lemon juice, sour chews, Brain-licker
These are sour things that rock my world.

The sweet sensation tickles my taste buds
Swings me round and round
Sour expression pops my ears and
Flies me up and down.

The Chinese use it at the corner shop
The best sweet 'n' sour thing is . . .
. . . Sweet 'n' Sour sauce.

Andrew Hill (11)
Sale Grammar School

Who Am I?

I feed on hatred and prejudice,
I can be called malevolent-minded,
I help to create death lovers,
My barbaric nature costs lives of innocents,
I am duplicitous and hate all humans,
I am like a poisonous spider,
Hanging in a web of fear and dread,
I am disguised as a friend whilst being a foe,
I am the Devil's devious weapon,
Dripping with bloodthirsty feats,
My ally is ignorance,
The evil that men do.

Liam Rumsey (11)
Sale Grammar School

Basketball: Heaven And Hell

Heaven is the greatest thing,
Hell is a poisonous sting.
Heaven is shooting hoops all day long,
Hell is getting beat by someone who plays ping-pong.
Heaven is winning by a hundred baskets,
Hell is all your team being put into caskets.
Heaven is slamming your basketball wish,
Hell is not getting an amazing swish.
But the worst thing of all,
Is finding out you're playing netball!

Mack Ashworth (12)
Sale Grammar School

Fire!

Fire! It spreads for miles,
It spreads for yards,
It spreads for metres,
It spreads to farms,
It spreads to forests,
It spreads to trees,
It spreads to barnyards
And the animals flee.

Fire! It destroys for miles,
It destroys for yards,
It destroys for metres,
It destroys the farms
It destroys the forests,
It destroys the trees,
It destroys the barns
And the animals flee.

Nicholas Lingard (12)
Sir Thomas Boteler CE High School

Fireworks

Fireworks!
Keep your pets indoors!
Leave them if they go under floors!

Bang! Bang! Off they go!
Beautiful sight, watch them glow!

Burning wood on the bonfire
Watching flames going higher and higher!

Bang! Bang! Off they go!
Beautiful sight, watch them glow!

Having fun with all your friends!
Don't get hurt or the party ends!

Bang! Bang! Off they go!
Beautiful sight, watch them glow!
Fireworks!

Shelley Meinen (11)
Sir Thomas Boteler CE High School

Autumn

Brown, orange, yellow and red,
Animals hibernating in bed.
Different leaves falling from trees,
So you can say bye to those buzzing bees.
Birds making big nest,
Conkers are falling, let's pick the best.
Brown, orange, yellow and red,
Shhh! The animals are hibernating in their bed.

Mia Edwardson (11)
Sir Thomas Boteler CE High School

Autumn

Autumn is the best part of the year
With the leaves falling and the animals hibernating
Autumn is different every year with new seeds blooming
All the animals are fast asleep
With a bundle of food sitting next to them.

Nathan Johnson (11)
Sir Thomas Boteler CE High School

Autumn

A ll the leaves falling off the trees.
U nderground, animals collecting food for hibernating.
T rees losing their multicoloured clothing.
U nsettled leaves like a carpet covering the universe.
M icroscopic insects getting buried in leaves.
N esting comfortably in the autumn air.

Laura Finch (11)
Sir Thomas Boteler CE High School

Autumn

A utumn is the time of year
when Hallowe'en and Bonfire Night are near
U nderneath the rustling trees there lies a lot of different leaves
T he weather changes, sometimes it's a hailstorm and
sometimes it's just a gentle breeze
U nexpected conkers fall, autumn is pretty great after all
M any animals hibernate and I think conkering is great
N ot many animals are awake
and it's freezing cold for goodness sake.

Darryl Cox (11)
Sir Thomas Boteler CE High School

Hallowe'en

H allowe'en is a time for the dead to come out of the grave.
A t Hallowe'en people get dressed up with scary masks
but they don't know there's really dead people out there.
L anterns are lit and pumpkins carved out
in the shape of scary faces.
L aughing demons and howling wolves all through the night.
O nly daylight can kill the demons, witches and ghosts
but there's another ten hours to go.
W itches flying around on sticks that fly around the night sky.
E veryone is scared to death when zombies pop out from the dead.
E veryone is happy when it is morning. Zombies, ghosts, demons
and witches go back to the dead.
N othing can stop the daylight coming until next year there will be
more scaring.

Joyce Hewitt (11)
Sir Thomas Boteler CE High School

Hallowe'en Night

H allowe'en is a scary night
A lot of people out to give you a fright
L iving alive
L iving dead
O n this night you may have no head
W itches out to give you a scare
E' verybody is everywhere
E verywhere you go you get a scare
N o wonder they call it Hallowe'en.

Alice Delooze (11)
Sir Thomas Boteler CE High School

Autumn

A utumn is the time when the leaves
start falling off the trees
U nder the night sky children come out
dressed in coats and gloves.
T umbling from the trees the leaves fall to the ground.
U mbrellas up as the rain falls from the sky.
M ountains of leaves which have fallen down from the trees.
N ovember brings fireworks and Hallowe'en.

Ben De Sanctis (11)
Sir Thomas Boteler CE High School

Autumn

A is for autumn when the leaves go all brown and crumbly
U is for foxes hiding under slides in the park
T is for trick or treating when they come to your door
U is for understanding autumn and why we have it
M is for migration when the birds travel south
N is for Bonfire Night with all the bangs and bombs in the night.

Dominick Salisbury (11)
Sir Thomas Boteler CE High School

Fiery Fingers

Fiery fingers are waiting for you,
Fiery fingers are red, white and blue.
Fiery fingers are scorching hot,
Fiery fingers are worth a shot.

Now it's over, they're about to cool down,
Fiery fingers are going to drown.

Fiery fingers can't wait to return,
The feeling inside makes my stomach churn!

Matthew Taylor (11)
Sir Thomas Boteler CE High School

Skipper's Song

Turn the rope,
    turn it high and low.
One short step
    and off you go.

Skip so slow,
    skip it so quick
Skip so soft,
    yes that's the trick.

So take it easy
    and keep it cool,
To stay the best
    at skipping school.

Zoe Dunning (11)
Sir Thomas Boteler CE High School

My Special Person

I am writing about the person who is special to me,
Amanda Whittaker,
She was my auntie Mandy,
She was more than my auntie,
A second mum,
I could talk to her,
I miss her,
She is no longer here,
She is in Heaven,
No more suffering for her,
She died New Year's Day 2003,
But the memory of her will carry on forever.
One day I will see her again,
In Heaven.
My auntie was very special to me.
Who is special to you?

Kirsty Vernon (11)
Sir Thomas Boteler CE High School

It's Winter

It's wintertime,
The weather is bad,
We are inside
And we are so glad.

In front of the fire,
Where we warm our feet,
Whilst we have
Something nice to eat.

The leaves are all gone,
The trees are looking bare,
We cannot see the birds anywhere.

It's all white outside,
Because it's been snowing,
We look inside
Where the fire is glowing.

The presents all
Under the tree,
Waiting there for
You and me.

We are so excited,
We just cannot sleep,
So we go downstairs
For one last peep.

Santa's been,
The presents are here
I got what I wanted
And gave a big cheer.

Robert Morris (11)
Sir Thomas Boteler CE High School

Man Utd

My favourite team is Man Utd,
I hate Liverpool,
Some say Man U are no good,
But I think they are cool,
Arsenal have Patrick Vieira
And Thierry Henry,
But soon you shall see,
We are not scared,
Because we're the devils in red,
You may see us in black,
Man U shall not hold back,
Ronaldo and van Nistelrooy are great,
King Keano is not a state,
Rio is a great defender,
Tim Howard is the best,
Giggsy is our winger,
The fans are Man U's guest,
Some say Nistelrooy's a diver,
But I just sing,
Nistelrooy's my king.

Phillip Green (11)
Sir Thomas Boteler CE High School

Dreams

A dream can be a fantasy it's only a few seconds long
It can be scary or it can be good, it can be a beautiful song
Before you go to sleep tonight think what your dream will be
Well rest your head and close your eyes and maybe you will see
I am sure your dream tonight will be a lovely sight
So the thing I say to you is don't let the bed bugs bite.
Goodnight.

Sarah Fox (12)
Sir Thomas Boteler CE High School

Winter

W inter is cold and great
I t literally sends shivers down your spine
N ot many people like waking up
T o find the floor
E ntirely covered with snow, so remember you won't see its
R ear for another year.

Samuel Wernham (11)
Sir Thomas Boteler CE High School

Dreaming

D reaming, dreaming, nightmare, dreaming.
R acing pulse, wake up screaming.
E verybody seems to be looking
A t night-time the fear is haunting
M eaning wanting not to go to sleep
I t's always there you can't escape it
N ever without your fear your nightmare
G oing nowhere just following you wherever you are
wherever you go it's there haunting you.

Deanna Ratcliffe (11)
Sir Thomas Boteler CE High School

Spiders!

The creepy-crawly cringy creatures
Go sliding in the bath
They slip and slide and twirl about
And happily have a laugh!
But when the humans have a shower
The happy spider screams
Then the water comes on
The spider is gone!

Kim Thackeray
Sir Thomas Boteler CE High School

Spooky Nights

Mist casting over the full moon,
Howling and prowling through the night,
The creatures will be arriving soon,
Werewolves and witches make you scream,
Wrap yourself in your sheets,
Can't sleep at all,
People screaming, shrieking,
Seeing things,
Spread your wings it's time to go,
Save yourself!

Siobhan Caulfield (11)
Sir Thomas Boteler CE High School

Bonfire Night

At Bonfire Night children are screaming with excitement
And all the rockets beaming,
Animals frightened, Catherine wheels tightened to the fence,
They cost more than a few pence,
Yes it's autumn time.
People enjoying themselves with all those fireworks from the shelves,
Keep pets safely away just for today.

Jason Brookes (12)
Sir Thomas Boteler CE High School

Bonfires

B ang! There goes a firework
O n the park, I am watching them
N ever go near the fire or a firework
F ears and terror of the animals
I t turns out very colourful
R emember, be safe because
E veryone could get hurt
S o everybody be careful.

Gemma Morris (11)
Sir Thomas Boteler CE High School

My Very Special Baby Sister

My sister is called Elle Rose Richards,
She is special to me because
She was born to come to me and my family,
She couldn't come to me and my family
But that was for a very special reason.
She is special,
Elle is very beautiful and could have surely been a model,
Even though we only met her when she was asleep,
You could tell she was the best baby in the world.
She is special,
She is now in Heaven with her angel friends,
Jumping from cloud to cloud,
Playing her golden harp!
Her and her friends playing hide-and-go-peek
Around the sunflowers in the garden!
We bought lots of things for a very special baby like Elle.
We all know she loves Winnie because
That was her first teddy.
We all love Elle!
She is special!

Kadie Richards (11)
Sir Thomas Boteler CE High School

Fire!

Fire! It spreads so quickly,
It crackles and spits
And burns so brightly in
The moonlit sky.

Fire! It's the deadliest
Thing in the world,
Though it can be very nice,
On a late Friday night,
When you light a fire
And watch your favourite film.

Julia Barber (11)
Sir Thomas Boteler CE High School

Frozen Winter

A twisted frozen blanket
Covering up the land.
Plants dying, but children
Laughing I don't understand.

Is that a tree I see?
Yes it is, with yellow sparkly lights,
When it is dark, and all in bed.
It would twinkle in the night.

Is that an overly large sock?
With some pretty toys inside,
Hanging on the wall,
With a bow that is tied.

A twisted frozen blanket
Melting on the land.
Plants growing but children,
Moaning I don't understand.

Ashley Shaw (12)
Sir Thomas Boteler CE High School

Winter

The night is cold and the bread has mould.
When I get up it will be stone-cold.
I got up to open my present
And there was a singing pheasant.
I went outside and took my sledge
And following me out was my dog called Pegs.
We played on the sledge
And had lots of fun.
Then a group of children
Came to the door
And started to sing.

Kathryne O'Brien (12)
Sir Thomas Boteler CE High School

Winter!

Where is the heat that warmed me up?
Where is the tweet of a blue tit?
Where is the sparkling water?
Has it all gone?

What is all this cold?
Where does it come from?
Why is the Christmas tree inside?
Has the sun died?

I remember Mr Snowman!
I know that Jack Frost!
I know what it's all about,
It's Christmas, thank goodness!

Lewis Seddon (12)
Sir Thomas Boteler CE High School

Moon And Stars

The stars twinkle in the night like big diamonds shining bright.
The moon is like a giant glowing banana.
The wind is warm, it makes you feel nice.
You can mistake an aeroplane's lights for coloured stars twinkling.
See a shooting star, your wish will come true.
The moon is our friend,
It shines all night long,
It is made of pearls
Or maybe even of diamonds,
Along with her friends such as the stars
Who shine all night,
Then the moon is cheerful and happy.
Goodnight!

Kathryn Laidler-Ball (11)
Sir Thomas Boteler CE High School

The Jolly Snowman

Snow is falling,
Hip hip hooray,
Mr Snowman's out to play,
With his long, orange nose
And his belly big and round,
You'll hear the children's laughter,
As the snow falls down to the ground.

Ian Cotterill (12)
Sir Thomas Boteler CE High School

War Around The World

(Dedicated to all the innocent people involved in any wars)

As they sit and wonder why,
Shall they live or shall they die?

Bombs and guns blasting everywhere,
Children are crying over there.

Soldiers fighting on different ground,
For a piece of the land from the world around.

Planes are flying in the skies above,
Food is rationed, but not the mother's love.

Lying in their beds to sleep at night,
Most people can't even switch on their light.

Dust and rubble flying everywhere,
But it seems that nobody cares.

Many different wars over the years have passed,
So please stop now and give everybody some peace at last.

Carrie-Anne Louise Latham (11)
Sir Thomas Boteler CE High School

Special!

Flowers will die,
The sun will set,
But you're a friend
I won't forget.

Your name is so precious,
It'll never grow old,
It's engraved in my heart
With letters of gold.

Rachel Anne Ward (11)
Sir Thomas Boteler CE High School

Autumn

A utumn is where the leaves fall
U nder the trees they lie
T ons of people get dressed up warm
U nder the stars people shiver
M oaning children have to stay inside
N early winter is upon us!

Chris Meacock (11)
Sir Thomas Boteler CE High School

Capricorn

C apricorn of power
A lways fight a battle
P owerful and fierce
R aging and grieving
I gnoring the pain
C onsidering it as nothing
O beying our command of life
R elief as the night falls
N ext, day arrives.

Sara Hughes (11)
Sir Thomas Boteler CE High School

Cats

Cats are playful,
Cats can scratch,
Cats chase mice and butterflies.

Cats bask in the sun,
Cats chase balls of yarn,
Cats fight in the alleyway.

Cats are ginger,
Cats are brown,
Cats are black and white.

Cats are tabby,
Cats are Persian,
Cats are tortoiseshell.

Cats are Siamese,
Cats are lynx,
Cats are tigers too.

Cats are long-haired,
Cats are short-haired,
Cats have matted fur.

Kittens are playful,
Lions are hunters,
But my favourite of all is the pussycat.

Victoria Fleming (11)
Sir Thomas Boteler CE High School

Stars

S hine upon the black night sky
T winkle with a long white cloud
A round all of the glorious things in life
R est upon a white cloud hanging above the world
S parkling with the sun as it leaves the land.

Simon Williams (12)
Sir Thomas Boteler CE High School

Families

Sometimes families are *amazing,*
Sometimes they get on your nerves,
Even though you love them,
You may have a little row.

Sometimes you can have a laugh,
Sometimes you can have a sob,
Maybe you can have a fall out,
But, you can always have a blast.

Families are loving,
Families always care,
Families are there for you when you fall down!
So never, never frown.

You know you love your family,
No matter what you do,
So remember to love your family
As much as they love you!

Nicolle Hackett (11)
Sir Thomas Boteler CE High School

The Weather Is Changing

The weather is changing
And so am I,
The weather is changing
I do not lie,
The weather is changing
It's getting cold,
The weather is changing
I'm growing old,
The weather is changing
And so am I,
The weather is changing
I'm going to die . . .

Hayley McCarthy (11)
Sir Thomas Boteler CE High School

Winter

W inter is coming with freezing nights
I cy cold days and nights
N o birds have been seen for days
T rees are bare of leaves
E veryone keeps wrapped up warm
R ain is not to be seen.

Michael Richard Ian Hoddy (11)
Sir Thomas Boteler CE High School

Summer

The sun is shining in the sky,
It's so nice when the weather is dry,
It's nice cos I can go out with my friends,
I never want the days to end.
I love to go out and play,
When the sun shines all day.
The weather man was right,
Cos he predicted the day would be bright.

Aimée Snape (11)
Sir Thomas Boteler CE High School

5th November

Fireworks light the sky as I am eating my Yorkshire pie.
When I am eating my treacle toffees my mum has a cup of coffee.
Bonfires blaze as I gaze at the starry sky.
Boxes vanish as fast as a cheetah, going for its prey.
Fireworks explode like a game on easy mode.

Adam McNeil (11)
Sir Thomas Boteler CE High School

Autumn

Autumn leaves are golden brown,
Twisting, turning to the ground.
The winter chill is locked away,
Away from those clouds of grey.

Although the summer has gone,
It will come again,
Bringing all things to life,
Taking away all pain.

Whoosh, bang, boom the fireworks go,
Landing where in winter will be snow,
People in woolly hats and gloves,
Eating toffee apple which I love.

Sasha Smith (11)
Sir Thomas Boteler CE High School

Hallowe'en

When Hallowe'en comes at night
Witches and ghosts
Give you a fright
When you see people lurking on the street
Too many people will ask you for trick or treat.

Hannah Peever (13)
Sir Thomas Boteler CE High School

The Wood Lady

The wood lady has a pointy hat that goes round and round,
With her beautiful nose and lips and her herring jacket
And her eyebrows and eyes carved just like a wood lady,
She looks like a queen.

Jade Simms (12)
Sir Thomas Boteler CE High School

Winter

In winter things begin to happen.
Icicles begin to form
And the nights become colder.

Xmas is drawing near
And children are getting excited.
But maybe on one winter's night,
Two inches of snow will fall.

For the next morning when the children wake,
They find the snow and rush out to play
In their PJs to make snowmen
And have a snowball fight all day long.

Darkness is falling and it's time to go in,
For the next morning is ahead.

Jade Louise Hunt (12)
Sir Thomas Boteler CE High School

Igloo Men

Igloo men are big and tall,
Some of them are very small,
They are big and fierce and they have a spear,
That is as long and sharp as a pier,
When they stab the fish they have a cheer,
Let's eat this fish because it is delish.

Igloo men are as fierce as a knight
And they like to wander at night,
They walk on the ice with big white coats,
As quiet as small white mice in a quiet boat,
They have wolves as fierce as a knife
And as protective as a man's life,
Winter is the coldest thing in the world
For an igloo man.

Lewis Herbert (12)
Sir Thomas Boteler CE High School

Wind

Breezy wind
Strong wind
Soft wind
Hard wind
Weak wind
Tough wind

Whistling wind
Howling wind
Squeaking wind
Roaring wind
Squealing wind
Screaming wind

Gentle wind
Strong wind
All winds!

Conor Steventon (11)
Sir Thomas Boteler CE High School

Warrior!

Warrior,
Blade shining,
His armour glittering like ice,
He wields his blade,
To attack!
He has returned.
Warrior
Beware!

Warrior,
Fighting mercifully.
The power of ten men,
As quick as the wind!
He has returned.
Warrior!
He has returned!

Lindsey Cannell (11)
Sir Thomas Boteler CE High School

The Ghosts And Ghouls!

It was a dark, stormy night,
The ghosts and ghouls were out of sight,
They were waiting to see who they could scare
And at last they could hear someone right there!

Just stood on the spot where they could see,
A lovely young girl, 'Just right for me!'
They pounce on her and grab her hair
And pull her right away from there!

They take her in and sit her down,
She had a horrible nasty frown!
Everything gets a little bit gruesome here
Time to have a rest as they put away their spear
And get ready for another *meal!*

Sara Connor (11)
Sir Thomas Boteler CE High School

Sports Day

Red, Black, Blue and Green,
All come out looking ever so mean.

The races begin,
Who's going to win
And go past the finish line?

Black had won,
Having loads of fun,
Holding the school cup trophy.

It was time to go home,
All the other teams would moan.

But Black had finally
Got *victory!*

Jordan Lawrence (11)
Sir Thomas Boteler CE High School

Football Poem

F ootball season starts
O n the pitch my heart is pounding
O n the pitch I can hear the crowd
T he ref blows the whistle to start the game
B ending the ball to the area
A wful it's a penalty
L ewis steps up to take the penalty
L ewis puts it in the bottom corner.

William Delooze (11)
Sir Thomas Boteler CE High School

Fredric The Jockey

Fredric the jockey,
Had a funny horse,
Who liked to gallop,
Round the course
And every day he'd go to a race
And win a trophy for his case.

Kane Phillips (11)
Sir Thomas Boteler CE High School

Football Goals

F oot hitting the ball
O nly he can score
O nly the goalie can stop it
T he crowd is going wild
B all is streaming through the air
A ll the crowd goes silent
L ast minute of the game
L ast goal is scored.

Shaun Gough (11)
Sir Thomas Boteler CE High School

Silky Snow

Silky snow-coloured stallion rolling in the grass.
Then gets up and starts to gallop.
With big feathers on his feet blowing in the breeze,
His long mane is blowing too in the heavy rain.
Then he goes in for shelter,
Out of the cold and into the heat.
Night-time comes he goes to sleep.
With his rug on he's nice and cosy.

Chelsea Margret Julie Goulden (11)
Sir Thomas Boteler CE High School

Tiger

T he time it spends in its hunting place
I t's waiting for its prey
G lancing around the field all day
E ver so quietly
R aahhh, it's caught it. The zebra's gore
And blood all over the grassy and muddy fields
He eats and starts the hunt again,
Raahhh!

Kirsten Done (11)
Sir Thomas Boteler CE High School

The Sea

The sea is like space, you float all night long
And race with the creature of the waters.
The whales make sounds like hounds that howl,
Whilst making their way to greet you
For your magical trip across the Atlantic Sea.
Yellow sunsets and ice-white waves,
Make you say, 'Oh what a sight.'

Laura Foster (12)
Sir Thomas Boteler CE High School

Will It Be The Same When I Come Back?

Will it be the same when I come back from outer space?
Will it be as friendly as it is now or will it be polluted with evil?
(Your decision)

When I go into outer space will there be pure air that I can breathe
Or will it be polluted with chemicals?

When I come back from outer space
Will I hate Earth or will I love Earth? (Your choice)
Keep your planet clean, love your planet.

Alice Francis (12)
Sir Thomas Boteler CE High School

Ice Cream

I ce cream is yummy for my tummy
C reamy and delicious
E xciting when I buy it

C reamy whippy ice cream goes in my mouth
R eally refreshing when I'm hot
E very flavour I do like
A nd on a cornet or in a dish it tastes nice with sauce on top
M elting, melting quick, quick, quick, I have to lick it before it drips.

Simone Ellis-Fox (12)
Sir Thomas Boteler CE High School

Trees Of Autumn

Snowmen form on the icy footpaths,
Snow falls form the dark blue sky,
Frost builds upon people's roofs,
Owls go out to hunt their prey,
Hedgehogs curl up to go to sleep,
Squirrels are collecting their nuts,
Leaves are falling on the ground.

Luke Kelly (11)
Sir Thomas Boteler CE High School

My Wish!

If I had one wish, what would it be?
There are so many things that I want to see,
So many things that I'd like to do,
What would you wish if it was you?
There's so much gloom in the world I'd stop,
What thing would best, what would be at the top?
War, hurting animals, racism all must end,
For this world to get better, and start to mend.
Racism is stupid, everyone's the same
We have the same colour blood, so this thing is lame.
We breathe the same air both day and night,
So we're all equal no matter if we're black or white
And why do we put animals through so much pain?
Hurting them to me seems cruel and insane.
They can't fight for themselves. We must help them to fight,
To give back the animals their special right.
And getting world peace would stop all war,
Because what is the point? What is it for?
We should love everyone, help the world to mend,
Then maybe the stupid thing called war would end.
So if I had one wish what would I choose?
'Cause if I choose one, the others would lose.
I could not decide, I like all three,
But with one wish, this cannot be.
So confused with what I would do,
So I ask again, what would you do if it was you?

Emma Clarke (11)
Sir Thomas Boteler CE High School

War

It was dark when men entered the battlefield,
Takers of life coming in different directions,
Life's stream flowing down the drain,
Swords trying to escape bodies,
Spirits trying to fly really high to the sky.

No more memories only graves.

Laura Ellison (11)
Sir Thomas Boteler CE High School

One Sunny Day

I look up into the clear blue sky,
The breeze is cooling me down,
The sun is shining,
Birds flying by.

The sea's waves lapping on the shore,
The rocks crumbling away each day,
A lighthouse shining its bright light,
Warning the boats away.

Scott Webb (11)
Sir Thomas Boteler CE High School

I'm So Popular

'I'm so popular,'
    Said the quiet girl
'I'm so popular,'
    Said the cool boy
'I'm so popular,'
    Said the naughty girl
'But I'm the coolest here.'
                                        Eeek!

Jenny Evans (11)
Sir Thomas Boteler CE High School

Elephant

The ferocious constantly prowling sea
Is an eager elegant elephant
Quickly eroding the cliffs,
Like an earthquake shaking
The rowdy, rough, ragged rocks,
The crude monster of depravity,
Is searching for creatures to conquer,
The boisterous, violent, turbulent intruder,
Carelessly churning the scared,
Innocent, saturated stones,
Just for satisfaction,
It rushes and stampedes
Up and down,
The sea is like an eager
Elegant elephant.

Jade Sutcliffe (11)
Sir Thomas Boteler CE High School

The Ghoul Under The Cupboard

I'm the ghoul under the cupboard
I sneak around at night
I watch your TV
And I mess with all your things
I'm the ghostly ghoul

I'm mean, I'm tough
I don't stand for anything
And then you brats come down
And then you ruin everything
Until another day.

Wesley Riley (11)
Sir Thomas Boteler CE High School

Autumn

Autumn is here
With the brown crispy leaves scattered everywhere
Where the wind is whistling and the trees are swaying
With winter near autumn is going
It's now getting cold outside
Autumn has gone.

Tom Mellor (11)
Sir Thomas Boteler CE High School

The Manor Ghost

The manor ghost is very creepy,
When it comes near you
It makes you very sneezy.

It knocks things over in
The middle of the night,
It even knocked over
A suit from a knight.

James Rowell (11)
Sir Thomas Boteler CE High School

Autumn Poem

A is for the animals that hibernate
U is for the most unusual weather that we have
T is for the trees that haven't got any leaves
U is for the umbrella weather that we have
M is for the masks that people wear for Hallowe'en
N is for the most brilliant nights like Hallowe'en and Bonfire Night.

Jennifer Roberts (11)
Sir Thomas Boteler CE High School

Autumn

In autumn,
Under your feet there's lots of crunching leaves.
The trees above are bare,
It's frosty and it's cold.
The lakes and ponds are ice, it shines in the light.
I stand and stare at the reddy-golden forest
As day becomes night.
The birds start to fly as it begins to rain,
It's autumn now, it's autumn again.

Jessica Lawless (11)
Sir Thomas Boteler CE High School

LFC

It was Owen running down the field,
Campbell chasing behind,
Lehmann strides out of goal,
Owen takes him on,
Campbell slides,
Owen goes down,
Penalty!
They shout,
Owen steps up, hits it,
Goaal!

Paul Burke (11)
Sir Thomas Boteler CE High School

Autumn

A utumn is when all the leaves fall off the trees
U sually you know when it is autumn cos leaves go crispy
T rees look empty in the cold night air
U nder things are animals hibernating
M is for migration
N o one knows how it is when all the trick or treaters come.

Nicola Thompson (11)
Sir Thomas Boteler CE High School

Poem About Me

C heerful, kind for others
H appy all the time
A ngry is not a word in her category
N ever selfish
T alented is what she is
E xcited all the time
L aughing all day long
L onely is what she does not like
E xtremely good.

Chantelle Whitmore (11)
Sir Thomas Boteler CE High School

The Bully

The ugly bully, the revolting bully,
Without the slightest clatter,
Jumps out from behind the tree
And gets ready to batter.

His fist shoots through the air,
As they sit down,
Then bonks some on the nose
And kicks them out of town.

He steals their money and takes their books
And yanks off their shoes,
Nicks their pencil case,
Then swipes their kazoos.

Marc Greenfield (11)
Sir Thomas Boteler CE High School

Hot Days

Look at the bright sky
Too bright to look at the sun
All hot and sweaty
Feeling like sunbathing
The sun making all tired
A good time to go swimming
Only a little breeze
Birds every morning singing on the trees
Sitting under the fans.

Josh Watson (11)
Sir Thomas Boteler CE High School

Fire

Is like a giant
munching,
crunching
throughout the leaves and trees.

Stay aware,
for fire is always near.

Whirring around
up the trees
and up the hills
till it meets
the end.

Abigail Betney (11)
Sir Thomas Boteler CE High School

Hallowe'en Night

H ailing through the night
A t night people get a fright
L ooping ghosts
L apping bats
O pening doors
W hat a night
E ating, trick or treating
E vening lamps, candles and pumpkins to light up the night
N o sunlight to brighten the night.

Christopher Dickenson (11)
Sir Thomas Boteler CE High School

Autumn

Autumn leaves are falling
Crunchy, crispy and brown

All the kids are disappearing
With a horrible frown

Now the weather is getting worse
The rain is lashing down

The lightning it's getting worse
The lightning thrashing down

The plants are dying
Fall to the ground

All plants are lying
Around.

Stephanie Cox (11)
Sir Thomas Boteler CE High School

Hallowe'en Night

H allowe'en is a scary night
A lot of people are very scared
L oads of frights
L oads of sweets
O n this night you do get scared
W hen the time comes you will have a fright
E veryone is scared
E verywhere you go you will have another fright
N o wonder they call it Hallowe'en.

James Herbert (11)
Sir Thomas Boteler CE High School

I Was . . .

I was the one who sat at the back,
I was the one who never spoke back.

I was the one who wore the wrong dress,
I was the one who was never the best.

I was the one who cried late at night,
Wondering and wondering why I wasn't right.

But I was the one who left the pack,
I was the one who never looked back.

Now I am the one who doesn't care if I'm cool,
Now I am the one who is nobody's fool.

Katie Griffiths (12)
Stockport Grammar School

Squirrels

Furry, flickering, never still,
Bouncing tails, with a fluffy frill.
One minute small and sweet,
The next, their minute feet
Scrabble on the tree bark,
Yet never leaving a mark,
Carrying birdseed or bread,
Giggling high above your head,
Dropping and throwing food,
Then abruptly changing mood,
To chase birds through the trees
Or drop low near cats, and tease
Until they screech and yowl
To scare the squirrels with their howl.

Curling in their nests as the cold draws in,
Huddled and sleepy, while the wind makes a din.
Each day hunting for some buried store,
Digging frantically, more and more.
Only to have humans chase them away,
Slinking back to their holes, and, day by day,
The creatures sleep the winter away.
Leaping up in spring, refreshed but thin,
Scavenging on bird tables, scrabbling through the bin.
A new generation of squirrels on the way -
To be born and fed, to steal and play.
Squirrels are born, and squirrels die,
No time for them to watch this all pass by.
More furry, flickering, never still,
More bouncing tails, with a fluffy frill.

Clare Wells (12)
Stockport Grammar School

New Girl

I dragged a comb through my wiry hair
And walked up the road to the school bus.
I just *wish* Mum would go away
And stop making such a fuss.

On the bus, I sit down on a dusty seat
And see other kids stop and stare.
I blush deep red and look away
But it's not *my* fault I've got bright ginger hair.

At school, people begin to accept me
As their new classmate.
I hope they don't see my sensitive side
Or I'll be the girl they can alienate.

I keep getting lost as I go to my lessons
And I bite my nails with worry.
Other students deliberately block my path,
Because they can see I'm in a hurry.

Phew! It's the end of school!
But which bus do I get on?
I look around for the one that goes to Wilmslow.
Could it have already gone?

I'm struggling with my maths homework
Inside my bedroom den.
My new school is *okay,* I suppose.
Should I come back again?

Natalie Ozel (12)
Stockport Grammar School

The Followers

The follower, the follower,
There's someone following me,
The follower, the follower,
They're running after me,
The follower, the follower,
I'm hiding behind a tree,
The follower, the follower,
They're gone as far as I can see,
The follower, the follower,
There's someone talking behind me,
The follower, the follower,
Goodbye, because now they've got me.

Gemma Medd (11)
Sutton High School

The Soldiers

Through the day and through the night,
There the soldiers lie and die.
From the bullets from the knife,
There the soldiers lie and die.
In their ears ring the screaming of
Innocent people dying but still
The soldiers lie and die.
In their tears lie the pictures
Of innocent people being slaughtered.
In fear and in pain but the soldiers lie and die.
Back at home their families lie in bed
Whilst their husbands lie and die.
When their families get told
They fall into the grass as if dying,
For the soldiers have died.

Kieran Pirie (12)
Sutton High School

I Hate School

I hate school it's so uncool,
Teachers yelling every day,
I can't be bothered with school today.

Why do they always shout at me?
Doing loads of work I do not agree,
Why do I have to go to school today?
I just can't wait until the end of the day.

I can't believe I've got maths today,
I have it nearly every day,
Finally last lesson I just can't wait,
Getting out of school it'll be great.

The bell is ringing I jump with glee,
It's the end of the day twenty-five past three.

Darryl Wright (12)
Sutton High School

I Want To Be . . .

I want to be a bird so I can
fly high and reach the sky

I want to be a tree so I
can swish and sway on a cold windy day

I want to be a star so I
can sparkle all night
you can only see me a little bit
because I am far, far away

I want to be a rainbow with
all the different colours on me
so when it rains and the sun comes
you'll see what I want to be

The only thing I want to be
is *me!*

Leanne Minshull (13)
Sutton High School

Cats

Cats stroll around
Whatever they do they will make no sound
Stalking around at night
They might even have a fight
They laze around in the sun
All they want to do is play and have fun
Cats like to chase birds and mice
They bring them home, that's nice
Jumping up on the bookcase
Carefully walking around
Without knocking anything down to the ground
Washing after breakfast, washing after tea
Looking after themselves so independently
We think we own them, but they own us
They only come near you when they want a fuss
Miaowing and purring for a treat
Most of all they like to sleep.

Carl Truman (13)
Sutton High School

My School

I love my school
It's so cool
I love my school
I never want to leave
All the memories I'm gonna receive
Whether they'll be good
Whether they'll be bad
As long as I'm never sad!

Lee Duffy (11)
Sutton High School

Homeless Child

I am as cold as a stone,
I look like a bare bone.

I am as starving as a stray dog,
I could eat food like a hog.

I am as smelly as an old shoe,
But I am as human as you.

I am as hated as a sewer rat,
But really I am as cuddly as a ginger cat!

Nicola Roberts (13)
Sutton High School

Bonfire Night

Remember, remember
The 5th of November
Bonfires roar
Fireworks boom.

Rockets go boom
In the night
Rockets go boom
And make a colourful sight.

Cartwheels spinning
Round, round, round
Cartwheels spinning
Make an awesome sound.

The guy on top
Burns to Hell
The guy on top
Lets off an awful smell.

Craig Edmondson (13)
Sutton High School

My Best Friend

My best friend, she's so cool,
My best friend, she's not a fool,
My best friend wants to be an actor,
My best friend doesn't want to be a dancer,
My best friend is so funny,
My best friend used to have a bunny,
My best friend likes Winnie the Pooh,
My best friend likes to say boo!
My best friend is so smart,
My best friend likes art!
That's my best friend!

Lauren Ellam (11)
Sutton High School

My Family

My family is loud and proud,
No matter where I am, I'm always found,
By that embarrassing crowd.

The old ones reckon they're hip and trendy,
Using words like minging,
Even when they're singing.

I wish when my mates came round
They'd be sound as a pound,
But they're not, they're still loud and proud.
How embarrassing!

My dogs they howl and growl,
They leave presents and they're always found,
Lying on the ground,
When it gets stuck to the bottom of your shoe,
You just wish it weren't you,
Especially when people start sniffing the air,
That's when you really start to care.

Beccy Dobbins (14)
Sutton High School

Liverpool

Liverpool are the best
They're better than all the rest
They score good goals
But also hit the poles

My favourite player's Steven Gerrard
I've been a supporter all my life

I hope they win the league
Maybe, I wish, please.

Kieran Fairclough (11)
Sutton High School

He Is

He is red like the blood in his body
He is a lion roaring in the Savannah
He is a cup of tea, warm and soothing
He is a wooden stool, hard and strong
He is a grill, burning hot.

Daniel Artell (13)
Sutton High School

Andy Griffs

He is black and white, moody and unpredictable
He is a pardrae, funny and stupid
He is Dr Pepper because he always drinks it
And he is fizzy and dark
He is a chair, old and tarty,
He is a bottle, bottles it up
And is going to burst.

He is Andy G.

Jack Jenkins (13)
Sutton High School

She Is . . .

She is a flower, my favourite object
She is pink, pretty and luminous
She is champagne, bubbly and cheerful
She is a baby bear, warm, cute and cuddly
She is a disco, exciting and lively
She is a soft chair, happy and comfortable
She is a drier, responsible and sincere.

She is my Auntie Tanya.

Danielle McFadden (13)
Sutton High School

Scratch From My Cat

I dream of escape to join the stars,
Have light from the moon, to heal my heart.
The blackness inside envelops my hope,
My dreams diseased - possessed by a ghost.
The twinkle of the stars catches my scars,
Brightening their luminous marks.
Slashed deep in my skin it's so hard to begin thinking of where to start.
When by the light of the moon I die, by the rise of the sun I'll live;
A blowing leaf in the wind - a shrinking cat from an offering hand,
I'll be where you are.
So miss me not for I will live in a different world to ours,
Where I will smile with no tears in sight,
Free from my intimidating scars.
And for once in my life a knife is a knife,
And a razor blade goes by its name,
Not a tool to display my hidden pain from each day,
Deep within my arms.
Until the night of the moon when you ask,
Once again what is that cut on your arm?
I'll reply with a smile and a careless glance down
That's just a mere scratch from my cat.

Nina Townson (17)
Sutton High School

Don't You Feel Bad?

Do you feel bad,
When you make people sad.
Will you always be the same,
Or will you just stand in shame?
Don't you care if you hurt someone?
One day they could even be gone.
What will you feel like if they died?
Maybe you wish you never tried.

Dean Brawn (11)
Sutton High School

It's Mean . . .

Just because I'm black they use me as a sack
And because of what I wear and my different coloured hair.
They skit me in my school and make me look like a fool.
They follow me to my home and throw eggs and ice cream cones.
I wish I was dead with the thoughts running through my head.

Josh Fowler (11)
Sutton High School

No Guts No Glory

'No guts - no glory!' is hammered into the men
Like the bullets they will fire
Like the orders and commands.

'No guts - no glory!' the saying that frightens them,
But what is glory when you've murdered?
What is it when you're dead?

Daniel Jones (15)
Sutton High School

My Life

I don't want to die,
Or get poked in the eye,
I would miss this place
And the human race.

I like my life,
It is cool,
My funniest happened in a pool.

When I was a baby,
I liked visiting places,
When I was four I learnt to tie my laces.

When I was young,
I drank nail varnish remover,
I woke up the next day lying next to a Hoover.

When I was young it seems,
Life was so wonderful,
A miracle,
So beautiful and magical,
All the birds in the trees they were singing so happily,
So joyfully, oh so playfully watching me.

Joel Tunstall (14)
Sutton High School

It

She is a dragon, ugly and mean
She is some lemon juice, sour and bitter
She is a lumpy chair, uncomfortable and awkward
She is a Monday, something no one looks forward to
She is a toaster, always pops up when you don't want her to
She is my *sister.*

Johnathan Paul Hadley (13)
Sutton High School

She Is . . .

She is yellow, bright and cheerful.
She is a rabbit, cute and cuddly.
She is tea, lovely to come home to.
She is a soft chair, brilliant and comfortable.
She is a wedding, happy and joyful.
She is my sister.

Michaela Walsh (14)
Sutton High School

She is . . .

She is . . .
Yellow, bright and helpful
She is . . .
A koala, nice and cuddly
She is . . .
A bottle of wine, lively and entertaining
She is . . .
A party, loud and exciting
She is . . .
A fireplace, warm and comfortable
She's *my mum!*

Jason Young (13)
Sutton High School

He Is . . .

He is blue lighting up the sky
He is a giraffe, always looking down on me
He is a cup of tea to keep me warm
He is a sofa, keeping me comfortable
He is my birthday, one of my presents.
He is my dad.

Michael Van Driel (13)
Sutton High School

I Am . . .

My name is enormous, massive and amazing,
I live in the heavens in the clouds with the twinkling stars
And the glowing moon,
I am as ancient as the Earth itself,
My brother is a hill, small but strong,
My sister is an Alp, pointy and sharp,
My enemy is the snow, icy and glimmering.

Rebecca Lookhart (11)
Sutton High School

I Am . . .

My name is big and destructive.
I can be found somewhere raven and rippled with light.
I am the creator of creation.
My brother is ice living a distance away.
My sister is the Earth so peaceful, dry and new.
My enemy is light when it waxes and destroys.

Georgina Anne Atkins (11)
Sutton High School

She Is . . .

She is a party, lively and colourful.
She is orange, warm and bright.
She is a big comfy armchair waiting for someone to cuddle.
She is champagne, bubbly and delicious.
She is a big cuddly bear, always up for a cuddle.
She is a knife, handy and always there when I need her.
She is my mum.

Melissa Manning (11)
Sutton High School

Useless

You're as useless,
As a stable without a horse,
As a curry without a sauce,
As useless as a river without any water,
As a person who is getting shorter.

You're as useless,
As a wig without a head,
As a room without a bed,
As useless as a clock with no hands,
As a lamp without any stands.

You're as useless,
As a pencil without any lead,
As a garden without any shed,
As useless as a bench without any wood,
As a person without any blood.

Laura Collins (12)
Sutton High School

He Is . . .

He is Easter, melting and yummy,
He is yellow, bright and warm,
He is a sofa, so soft and comfortable,
He is a knife, so handy and sharp,
He is champagne, so bubbly and fizzy
He is a lion, so cute and cuddly, but fierce.

Stephen Fletcher (12)
Sutton High School

Bullies

Me and my friend want to go to the moon
We're going to get there by flying in a balloon
We don't like bullies!

Me and my friend want to go to the moon
We've sussed how to get there flying in a balloon
We don't like bullies!

Me and my friend want to go to the moon
I wish I was at home watching telly
All the bullies call us smelly!

We don't like bullies!

Lauren Pearson (12)
Sutton High School

The Painting On My Wall

The golden sun's reflection lights up the mighty river
As it sparkles with life as the seagulls fly overhead.

Upon the bank was the long grass waving
In different colours as the sun sets
Palm trees and oak trees move with the gentle breeze.

As the sun sets, clouds cover the sky
To make way for the coming night
This is my painting on my wall
My ideal dreamworld
My Heaven.

Mark Kavanagh (16)
Sutton High School

I Am . . .

My name is ancient and hot,
I am sweltering and decaying with my own immense heat,
My brothers are smaller but just as hot as me,
My sisters are the peaceful mountains
Their brims touching the peak of the sky.
I have no enemies because I fear no one,
Everyone trembles at my feet.

Ben Moore (12)
Sutton High School

I Am . . .

My name is scolding and tumultuous,
I live on islands and where it is hot.
I am hot and I sometimes blow. If I blow you will know.
My sister has a sweet, loving nature.
My brother is horrible rain,
My enemy is a tornado, fast and ruining my land,
I am a . . . *volcano.*

Ryan Bello-Baamonde (11)
Sutton High School

I Am . . .

My name is slippery and tall.
I live in water, in the northern and southern hemisphere.
I am frosty and from the past, tied to the future.
My brother is close to my sister.
My brother is a glacier, frosty and white.
My sister is the sea, cold and deep.
My enemy is the copper sun rippling with light.
Can you guess what I am?

Scott Wotton (11)
Sutton High School

He Is . . .

He is a mouse, small and so tiny
He is a funeral, so dull and so sad
He is a soft couch, so lovely and comfortable
He is a washing machine, so clean and so soft
He is a bear, so strong and so fizzy
He is a cheetah, so fast and so sneaky.
He is my dad.

Daniel Parsonage (11)
Sutton High School

I Am . . .

My name is tall and fair
I live on the ground and air
I am as old as the Earth, I am the past
Present and hopefully the future
My enemy is the rain, it will erode me and
Wear me away but I will survive because
There is more snow than rain.

James Stewart (11)
Sutton High School

She Is . . .

She is a party, so lively and on the move.
She is red, a bright lovely colour.
She is a couch, soft and bouncy.
She is an oven, so slow.
She is Coca-Cola, so cold.
She is a tiny little ant who has a say in nothing.
She is my sister.

Sam Toy (11)
Sutton High School

She Is . . .

She is . . .

She is a party, rushing around and in the way.
She is the colour black, mucky and ugly.
She is a worn out sofa, all lumpy and uncomfortable.
She is a pan, greasy and hot.
She is a load of sprouts, horrible and soft.
She is a buffalo, moody and disgusting.
She is my sister, horrible and stubborn.

She is . . .

She is a wedding, cheerful and happy.
She is the colour red, busy and around.
She is an armchair, really comfy and welcoming.
She is a knife, really sharp and helpful.
She is a bottle of shandy, fizzy and fun.
She is a cheetah, speedy and everywhere.
She is my mum, really nice and always there.

Dale Jonathan Cotton (11)
Sutton High School

I Am . . .

My name is sleek, sweet and fluorescent,
I am found anywhere in the world from
Icy cold summits to warm sticky deserts.
I am from the past, present and the future,
My brother is a gigantic rainforest with his huge strong trunks.
My sister is a swaying palm tree, with her huge emerald leaves.
My enemy is the sun.
It makes me wilt.

Laura Jordan (11)
Sutton High School

I Am . . .

My name is the grass blowing in the wind,
I am as young as the old.
My brother is an erupting volcano,
My sister, she is as calm as a lake,
My enemy is a waterfall crashing down on the rocks.
I am . . .
        That's a secret.

Chris Newman (11)
Sutton High School

He Is . . .

He is thunder, mad and moody
He is red, scary and fast
He is uncomfortable like a rock
He is a spoon, easy to break
He is a burger, easy to put away
He is a monkey, active and cheeky
He is always energetic

He is my brother . . .

Clinton Ross (11)
Sutton High School

Someone Special

She is someone special in my life
Me and my friends think that she is kind
She is someone who we really like
I like to say so much about her
She is so good, she makes my car purr.

Bethany J McLoughlin (11)
Sutton High School

My Friend My Dog

My friend listens to me,
My friend doesn't argue back,
My friend doesn't mind when I make mistakes,
My friend is my dog.

My friend protects me,
My friend plays with me,
My friend shares his toys,
My friend is my dog.

My friend likes food,
My friend likes chewing,
My friend has got sharp teeth,
My friend is my dog.

My friend is always there,
My friend is cheerful,
My friend is the best,
My friend is my dog.

Chanel Goff (12)
Sutton High School

Football

Football is the best,
The players have important guests.

Liverpool are the best,
Everyone has a sweaty vest.

Players can take any pain,
In any game.

When Liverpool win the crowd goes wild,
Except for the losing team of a child.

Chris Ellery (11)
Sutton High School

Myself

I am funny,
I am a daredevil,
I am sporty,
I am mad,
I am greedy,
I am happy,
What are you?

I've had this poster
For years and years . . .
It's stuck on my wall and I've had it
For years and years . . .
It looks like it stares at me,
For years and years and years . . .

Mathew Hall (11)
Sutton High School

My Friend

My friend is funny every day
My friend is cheerful in every way
She is the best at making me laugh
She can also be quite daft
We always have a great time
And we're both friendly and cause no crimes
We both have a friend called Amy
And in drama she brought a photo in of
When she was a baby.

My friend is crazy
But she's not lazy
Her name is Danielle
And she is my best friend.

Charlotte Anne Hartshome (12)
Sutton High School

Jack

Jack is a happy boy,
Oh, he is filled with joy.
Jack always jumps in the air,
He flies up to the air.

But oh, his joy goes,
Big bullies punch his nose.
They give him bad grief,
Like a bit of cow beef.

But he always gets better,
With a fully apologised letter.
The bullies soon feel sorry
And in his honour they break a lorry.

Jack forgives them,
Makes friends with them,
All from then on,
The boy is protected until he is gone.

Christopher Jennings (11)
Sutton High School

Dolphins

Dolphins
Dolphins swimming in the sea
Splashing around with pride and glee.

Dolphins
Dolphins eating all the fish
To swim with you would be my wish.

Dolphins
Dolphins so many tricks we could do
If only my wish would come true.

Laura Ball (14)
Sutton High School

Strawberries

Strawberries are sweet,
Strawberries are cool,
They don't taste nice in a swimming pool,
If you don't like them,
Well that's just you,
Well if you do
Please say *woo hoo hoo.*

Jessica Marsh (11)
Sutton High School

Autumn

Leaves are falling,
The cold is here.
Winter is calling,
It's that time of the year.

Down comes the rain,
I can feel the cold.
The wind whips me like a cane,
I feel so old.

In come the dark nights,
Fires are heating.
On with trousers and tights,
The weather's defeating.

Crisp, crunchy, slipping and sliding,
Red, yellow, orange and green.
I look up and the sun is still hiding,
The cold is back and once again to be seen.

Autumn is here,
Summer has gone.
When will the skies be clear?
Look in the sky where the sun once shone.

Natalie Youd (15)
Sutton High School

Hate

The hate, it builds inside me
Like a demon trying to escape
It eats at my body from within
Turning my heart to black
No remorse for anyone
I'll spend my life alone.

The hate, it pulses inside me
The demon has nearly escaped
It slashes through my organs
Eats away through all my flesh
It snaps my bones one by one
My body crumbles to the floor.

The hate, it explodes out of me
The demon can escape
The evil beast is free in the world
Who will its next victim be?
An innocent victim unknowing of their fate
Death crawls upon them
There is no escape.

Jenni Higgins (17)
Sutton High School

The Man Who Lived In A Tree

Once, there was a man
Who lived in a tree
He never worked
He only ate leaves
He never left
He always stayed at home
He had no TV
He had no phone.

Ryan Caswell (12)
Sutton High School

Hallowe'en

The cackling of the old witch,
The purring of the cat.
The potion that she put
On the poor black bat.

The crying of the baby,
As it wakes up.
The sipping of my mum,
Drinking from her cup.

The calling of the register,
In the afternoon.
Then it comes to night-time,
When the cow jumps over the moon.

Then I read my favourite book,
It's called 'Harry Potter'.
Then someone screams,
'Ha, now I've got ya!'

Terri Parker (12)
Sutton High School

War In Iraq!

People killing, people dying,
Children sleeping on the streets.
Bombs flying past
And going off not far away
From what they call home.
The only thing these children have,
Is the people surrounding them.
The world would be such a better place,
If people and countries were friends,
Not enemies.

Sadie Diamond (12)
Sutton High School

Football Crazy

Heskey is running
Up the pitch,
He has a shot . . .
Goal!

Liverpool are leading
1-0 up, Everton has got the ball,
They've passed the halfway line.
Rooney has a shot and he misses.
We don't believe he missed
An open goal.

Beep, the half-time whistle
Has just gone.
Five minutes later
The whistle goes
For the second half.

This time it's Radinski
Who has a shot . . .
Goal!

All you can hear is booing
Around the Anfield stadium.

There are 10 seconds left.

Owen has the ball,
He shoots, he scores,
Now there's cheering
Around the Anfield ground.

The match ended
Liverpool 2, Everton 1.

Connor Rogers (12)
The Heath Specialist Technology College

The Sea

The sea is like an angry dog
Snarling and growling as it wastes away the golden sand.
The sky is like a grey and black bear
Roaring at the sound of thunder
Then lightning comes
But almost suddenly a ray of sun shone down
With a white sky like the fur of a polar bear's skin.
The sea is like an angry dog.

Amy Carlton (11)
The Heath Specialist Technology College

The Dentist

Waiting
Dreadfully waiting
For the man to shout my name.

Will it be now?
Will it be later?
A scream from behind the wall.
His victim then walks out,
With a tear and a drop.
My turn soon!
A chair,
A man,
There it was, the name,
My name!
'Stephanie,' she shouts.
She shouts it again, 'Stephanie.'
It went through my head.
Oh no, it's been called out.
I see the chair, I see the man,
I curl up, walking,
Just then I hear,
'Open wide!'

Stephanie Shaw (11)
The Heath Specialist Technology College

Dentist!

Waiting . . .
Waiting . . .
I think I'm going mad!

Sitting there . . . tick-tock
Tick-tock . . . still waiting
Screams from the walls
As the drill buries itself in the mouth of another victim . . .

Then I hear those dreaded words . . . 'Next please . . .'

I turn . . .
I run . . .
I stop . . .
I cry . . .
I scream . . .
I plead . . .
I beg . . .
I sit . . .
He starts . . .
He finishes . . .
And says, 'That wasn't too bad, see you in 3 weeks!'

Elliott Rowe (11)
The Heath Specialist Technology College

Stars

A star is sparkly
In the summer
In the sky
Warm weather
Wearing the black sky
Sitting above us
Astronomy!
Romantic dinner to watch them with.

Ashley Roberts (13)
The Heath Specialist Technology College

The Dentist

Sitting,
Sitting in the dreadful room
Waiting for the dentist woman,
To shout my name!

Will it be now?
Will it be ever?
I don't want to do it!
Not now! Not ever!
A scream, a shout
It's me, it's me soon.

I'm still waiting,
But now I hate it
'Hayley,' she shouts.

Oh no, my name, it's been read out,
I'm scared to shout, it's been read out!

I went upstairs to sit in the chair,
I want my mum
I want to go,
Please,
Please,
Let me go!

Hayley Whitehead (11)
The Heath Specialist Technology College

The Dentist's Chair!

I'm waiting here, I'm a nervous wreck,
I'm fearing that she'll call me next,
I really don't want my tooth taken out,
I feel like I want to scream and shout!
Oh no, here goes, she said my name,
I never want to come here ever *again!*

Emily Louise Hanrahan (12)
The Heath Specialist Technology College

Trapped

Trapped . . .
Trapped . . .
I think I'm going mad
Strange yells crawling down the corridor
The closer it gets the weirder I become

Suddenly my name is called through the halls
It . . .
Echoes
Echoes
Footsteps drawing . . .
Closer
Closer
People
Crying
Wailing
Everything
Fading
Fading
Fading . . .

Luke Hope (11)
The Heath Specialist Technology College

Holiday

The golden sand shining in the sun
as I walk onto the beach.
The beach was bare, nobody to see
as I get out my towel
The cliff begins to sway back and forth
as I lie down, the seagulls screech,
The waves crashing softly from a passing boat
and the club music from the hill
All the hours fly by, listening to the children
playing in the water.

Mark Turnross (11)
The Heath Specialist Technology College

I'm Not That Different

Hurt and lonely,
Isolated with pity,
Stares and whispers,
Problemed and little.

I'm not that different!
I'm not that different!

I've got no control,
Can't look in the mirror,
I'm lonely and distorted,
People glare in horror.

I'm not that different!
I'm not that different!

People should accept me,
I know I do,
I'm no different inside,
Just the same as you.

Jennifer Webster (13)
The Heath Specialist Technology College

I've Run Away From Home

I've run away from home,
Now I am all alone,
I've ended up in Heathrow airport,
Dragging giant dragons down departures,
Me and my mates have parted,
Departures looks like a graveyard,
So cold and deserted,
The harsh lights scream into my ears
While I bring out my tears
So I wish I had never left my home.

Jade Smith (14)
The Heath Specialist Technology College

England Vs Brazil

He has the ball
Now passes it on to the wing
Runs down with pace
And . . . crosses it in

It's a free header
And hits the post!

Now the opposition are
Racing down the pitch
Beckham has been fouled in the box
And it's a . . .
Pen!

Owen steps up and shoots
It's a . . . *goal!*

Brazil kick off
It's Rivaldo with a shot from the halfway line
It's curling in
Goal!
What a goal by Rivaldo
And he has put them back on level.

England kick off
And only 10 minutes to full-time.

Time's now ticking
The referee blows his whistle
Full-time!

Now extra time has begun
Brilliant play by both teams
Full-time in extra time
Now the dreaded pens.

1st pen for Brazil is Rivaldo, he shoots, it's a goal!
1st pen for England is Owen, he shoots, he misses!

Rivaldo puts it in easily
Gerrard hits it over the stadium.

It's now Ronaldo and he scores.
Beckham has missed.

Brazil have won.

Kevin Boardman (12)
The Heath Specialist Technology College

As I Look Into The Mirror

As I look into the mirror
I get a shiver
Now it's time for dinner
Why me? Why me? Why me?

Every day I wake up
I try to cover my face with make-up
But people can still see
The disfigurement on me
Why me? Why me? Why me?

I have lots of friends on the phone
But in the yard I stand alone
Now it's time to go home
Why me? Why me? Why me?

Don't people think or care
When they stop and stare
My disfigurement I cannot hide
What about my feelings inside
Why me? Why me? Why me?

Lalah Smith (13)
The Heath Specialist Technology College

Why Me?

Everyone's staring
What's wrong with me?
Maybe it's others with the problem
But all I can think is . . .
Why me?

I feel so lonely
I'm on my own
No one wants to know me
I'm all alone.
Why me?

Why am I different?
I should be the same
I wish it was over
And I was normal again.
Why me?

It's not my fault
I couldn't help it.
If only I could turn back time.
I would try and not be like this.
Why me?

As I look in the mirror
I just feel pale
I wish I was normal
And just the same.
Why me?

I wish I had control
And could change how people are so mean
But they won't change
It's how they've always been.
Why me?

Emma Vine (13)
The Heath Specialist Technology College

Argh! The Pain

I have no way,
No how,
No way,
I won't ever change back.

Oh the pain, the pain, the pain
Don't stare at me in worry,
I will bounce back
No hurry.

Am beautiful,
Not.
I have burns all over my face
Am not happy.

Oh the pain, the pain, the pain
Don't stare at me in worry,
I will bounce back,
No hurry.

I can't get a job,
Because they look at me in . . .
Horror
Why me, why me?

Elizabeth Robinson (13)
The Heath Specialist Technology College

Don't Cry For Me

Don't cry for me,
I'm only human.
When I walk down the street,
You stare,
Why do you stare?
Everyone is unique,
So why do you make me feel lonely?

I'm not so different,
I'm just human,
So please don't stare,
So please don't stare.

As time goes on,
I think to myself,
I am not the one with the problem,
You're the one with the problem.

I'm not so different,
I'm just human,
So please don't stare,
So please don't stare.

I wish I had control
And could change how people stare,
But I can't change that,
So please don't cry for me.

Nick Ridgway (13)
The Heath Specialist Technology College

Beauty Doesn't Count

I cannot turn back,
No way,
No how,
I have got no self control!

I am deformed but I don't care,
My face is destroyed everywhere,
But I don't care,
Everyone can stare!

It's what's inside that counts,
Not the pain on the outside that begins to mount,
But everyone can stare,
Because I don't really care!

I can't bear to look in the mirror,
I can't bear to see my reflection,
But I can cope with it,
So why can't you!

I'm still the same as you,
If I could go back I would,
If I could fix it I would,
I could do anything you could,
I'm still human!

Because beauty isn't everything in this world!

Chloe O'Rourke (13)
The Heath Specialist Technology College

Why Me?

I look in the mirror
Oh God!
Why me?
Why me?

I go to the supermarket
People stare at me.
Why me?
Why me?

I do my shopping and reach the till,
The checkout girl just stares.
Why me?
Why me?

I run out the shop
Leaving my shopping behind.
Why me?
Why me?

I don't stop 'til I reach my house,
I slam the door shut.
Why me?
Why me?

'Surprise!' shout my family and friends.
Oh God!
I forgot it was my birthday!

People do care,
I don't care what you think, so there.

Claire Knight (13)
The Heath Specialist Technology College

In The Shadows

I cannot look in the mirror
As the person who is staring back
Is different to who I am.
My world has changed
I used to be a beauty
But now I am different.

Why me?
Did I deserve this?
Was it my fate?
Was it my fault?

I stay in the shadow
Behind each person I am near.
If I don't stay behind the shadow
People will stare, look down on me.
I have no control,
I am different.
Why me?
Did I deserve this?
Was it my fate?
Was it my fault?

I am different but only on the outside,
But it's the inside that counts.

Ruth Kingsley (13)
The Heath Specialist Technology College

Looking In The Mirror

Looking in the mirror
Burns everywhere
Scars cut so deep
Why me? What did I do wrong?
Can't someone change this?
I would do anything.

Looking in the mirror
Seeing my ugly, deformed face
It hurts so bad
Why am I so different?
Why do they stare?

Looking in the mirror
At the person staring back.
People stare all the time
What's wrong with them? I think.
Why are they staring? Stop it! Go away!
Leave me alone, beauty doesn't matter.

Oh the pain, the pain, the pain,
Don't stare at me in worry,
I will bounce back,
No hurry.

Stop gasping at me.

Yasmin Ismail (13)
The Heath Specialist Technology College

Disfigurement

If you disfigure your face
You feel disgraced
And the people around you
Think you're from a different race.

You're not alone
So don't go and moan
The community is with you
Friends and family too.

Don't let your looks bother you
That goes to all the other disfigured in the world too
You will get a scare
When people stare
But take no notice and you will be getting there.

If you are disfigured don't be ashamed
Then you will pull through and you'll not hear a name
You will have to learn if it was crash or burn
For all the others in the world you'll have to wait your turn.

James Hassall (13)
The Heath Specialist Technology College

Looking In The Mirror

Look in the mirror,
And see your true self,
Ignore the burns,
Forget your horror,
Look in the mirror,
You're no different,
Get rid of your loneliness,
Be brave,
Be strong and then . . .
You look in the mirror,
And it's not so bad,
You're still beautiful
Just keep telling yourself that!

Janine Durr (13)
The Heath Specialist Technology College

Not Me

You all think that beauty's it,
People think your face must fit,
The people standing all around,
As beautiful as one million pounds.
Look in the mirror and then you'll see
You are lucky you're not me.

But what if your face was scarred and burned,
And people stared, didn't say a word.
Your life would be ruined, just a mess,
Unless you look in the mirror
And then you'll see,
You're lucky, you're not me.

Little Tom, he played with fire,
He shouldn't have gone near that wire,
It scarred, burned and ruined this face,
It had changed it out of place.
Look in the mirror and then you'll see
You're lucky, you're not me.

Tom looked in the mirror and then he said,
'Why didn't I stay home in bed?
Now look at me and my ribbon face,
It completely moved out of place.
Why me? Why me? Why couldn't it be you?
Then he started to cry, 'Boo hoo.'

Maybe this will teach you not to stare,
If you keep doing this you're going nowhere,
Talk to them, then you'll see
It's beyond the face, the person be.
Look in the mirror and then you'll see
You're lucky, you're not me.

Kristian Harvey (13)
The Heath Specialist Technology College

Come Outside

What are you doing being sat at home?
Come outside and stop being alone,
Don't be scared to come outside
You can't stay at home and hide inside,
If faces are looking
And eyes are staring
Just ignore them don't be shy.

Look in the mirror
Stop looking at me,
Look at your beauty
There's plenty to see.

What are you doing being sat at home
Come out and stop being all alone,
Just come outside, don't be shy
If people look
And people stare,
Just ignore them, just look like you don't really care
Just remember to hold your head high in the air.

Look in the mirror
Stop looking at me,
Just believe in yourself
There's not much difference between you and me.

Natalie Hankers (13)
The Heath Specialist Technology College

Beauty Doesn't Matter

Looking in the mirror,
Oh what a disgrace,
Why me? Why not someone else's face?

Oh the pain

Looking in the mirror,
What a shame,
Why do I have to go through with this pain?

Oh the pain

Looking in the mirror,
Seeing the burns all over my face,
God why are you putting me in this place?

Oh the pain

Looking in the mirror,
Do you know how it feels?
People staring at you all the time,
I feel like saying is it a crime? No,
Because beauty doesn't matter.

Laura Gavin (13)
The Heath Specialist Technology College

Untitled

It's nearly time for my holiday
sitting in the sun
swimming in clear blue seas
drinking soft smoothies
walking on sun-kissed sands
groovin' in jumpin' bars
eating tropical treats.

Lee Fisher (13)
The Heath Specialist Technology College

Why Me?

People always staring
And also glaring
So I feel upset
So I cuddle my pet
He doesn't care
And looks and stares.

Why me?
Why me?

I get turned down
For jobs and dates
And I don't have loads of mates
So treat me the same
Because I'm in pain

Why me?
Why me?

All I ask for is for you
Not to stare and not to gaze
Because I want to be treated the same.

Why me?
Why me?

David Garbutt (13)
The Heath Specialist Technology College

Look In The Mirror, Don't Look At Me

Look in the mirror
Don't look at me
We're not so different
You're just obsessed with beauty
All you do is gaze
I don't like being like this

Look in the mirror
Don't look at me
Try and look past the burns
There is a person inside of me
Beauty isn't everything
Most people see straight past me

Look in the mirror
Don't look at me
That woman and man see me
I wonder if they feel lonely
Look they have the same burns
Most people don't realise how hurt I am

Look in the mirror
Don't look at me
Children stare a lot
Some even have the quick whisper
I was put in this position
Why me?

Carla Fisher (14)
The Heath Specialist Technology College

Face

If you feel so lonely
Don't feel left out
Don't feel you're different
So don't feel that you're the only one crying out

Beauty isn't everything
So don't feel left out

If you're scared
Don't hide away
If you can't bear to be looked at
Don't hide away

Beauty isn't everything
So don't feel left out

I want you to look me in the face
So nothing's different or bad about me
Some people can be cruel and harmful
And others can be so kind and warm

Beauty isn't everything
So don't feel left out.

Tim Felton (13)
The Heath Specialist Technology College

The Moon

The moon is round and silver
It is the winter
Up in the sky
Still very cold
Wearing a velvet blanket
Up and up goes the silky staircase
While the nights get thinner
The man in the moon is eating his lonely dinner.

Sarah Dean (12)
The Heath Specialist Technology College

Abused And Confused

Don't let me lose you
I'm not trying to confuse
Until I shoot through you
And tell you why I got the boot out of school
The teachers abuse me and try to confuse me
Still I feel like muck
Getting wound up then getting put down again
I try and tell my mum but she just acts dumb
The teachers get away with it
I just stay with it
I need to get away from this destiny
Those teachers say I need to relax
But they should just go and get waxed
To put up with the pain and realise
That they're so vain.

Ricky Dundon (13)
The Heath Specialist Technology College

Forget About Disfigurement

Not looking like anyone else
Is not making me feel sorry for myself
Saying this all the time
Keeping disfigurement out of this rhyme

'Why are you staring?' I ask
Not so different as I pass
Saying this all the time
Keeping disfigurement out of this rhyme

People stare
Do I care?
Saying this all the time
Keeping disfigurement out of this rhyme.

David Clare (13)
The Heath Specialist Technology College

Beauty Is Not Everything

Beauty is not everything
Walking down the street people stare
At my face but what for?
I'm no different on the inside
It's just the outside that's different

Beauty is not everything

I look in the mirror
All I see is hate
What happened to me?
Why me?

Beauty is not everything

People pity me
But what for?
I feel isolated
Trapped in my own little world

Beauty is not everything

People don't see me
They see the disfigurement
The only emotion I feel is pain

Beauty is not everything.

Amy Booth (13)
The Heath Specialist Technology College

Yesterday

Yesterday was . . .

Yesterday was sad and gloomy
Yesterday was happiness and smiles
Yesterday was dark and wet
Yesterday . . .

Today is mean and terror
Today is cloudy and misty
Today is spooky and bloody
Today . . .

Tomorrow will be lonely and frowns
Tomorrow will be scary and chilly
Tomorrow will be breezy and dry
Tomorrow . . .

Sad, madness
Gloomy, terror
Misty, happiness
Cloudy, smiles
Mean, darkness
Bloody, wetness
Scary, breeze
Chilly, dryness
Lonely, frowns.

Matthew Hayes (12)
The Heath Specialist Technology College

Liverpool Vs Everton

The game kicks off
Owen running with the ball.
He passes to Heskey
Passes to Gerrard
Knocks it past more players,
Now he shoots, it's a great save.
The Everton keeper throws it out
Rooney picks it out on the halfway line
Takes it past one,
He shoots,
But misses.
Ten minutes have passed.
Liverpool take the centre
As time passes
Liverpool get another goal
Two to none.
As players walk off the pitch
Some sad
Some happy.

Lewis Buckley (11)
The Heath Specialist Technology College

The Finger

Yesterday I had a bit of a fight,
My finger got cut off with a knife.
Today I got a false one, it hurt,
The operation I mean.
Tomorrow I will have forgotten,
That I got a bit mad with a knife.

Chris Newall (13)
The Heath Specialist Technology College

The Longest Wait Ever

Tick-tock
Waiting
Doing
Nothing
Else
The pale
White walls
Seem
To be
Turning
Red with
Blood
Tick-tock, rattle goes the lock
The door slowly turns
The masked surgeon walks in
'Count to ten,' the surgeon said.

1
2
3
4
5
6
. . .

Jordan Mather (11)
The Heath Specialist Technology College

My Day At The Dentist

Still waiting for the dentist to call my name,
I don't want to go,
I want to go home
Please let me go home.

Still waiting,
Soon she is about to call my name,
At this moment she called out my name, 'Sarah.'
I went in very terrified,
I got onto the chair very slowly and screeched.

My mum said, 'It's your turn.'
'I don't want to go in,
I don't want to go in.'
The dentist said to me, 'Open your mouth.'

I don't want to,
I don't want to,
I opened my mouth slowly.

Sarah Olcell (11)
The Heath Specialist Technology College

Yesterday Was . . .

Yesterday was sunny drizzle
Today is cloudily quietness
Tomorrow will be windy delightfulness.

Yesterday was damp coldness
Today is dry thundery
Tomorrow will be light dank.

Yesterday was slippy fun
Today is sickly misery
Tomorrow will be joyful smiles.

Michael Highton (12)
The Heath Specialist Technology College

The Needle

Waiting
Still waiting
Waiting to go into the dark, cold room
Waiting for them to call my name
I hope it is not soon
I hope not
I can hear the whimpers from behind the wall
I can hear the patients cry.
I'll be next
I'll be next
    Tom
        Smith
            Tom
                Smith
It's my turn
My . . .
My turn for the needle
My turn to go the dark, cold room.

Daniel Mainwaring (13)
The Heath Specialist Technology College

The Great Sausage Escape

I opened the freezer
Then a sausage ran out
I tried to catch it
There was no way out
Then I slammed it in the frying pan
It started to squeal
But I had no mercy
And shoved it in my mouth.

James Knight (13)
The Heath Specialist Technology College

Runaway

I've ran away from home
Oh, no I'm all alone.
There's no going back
And I didn't even pack
The walking is hurting my feet
Right now I could do with some heat
It's cold and dark here outside
But I can't help but shiver inside.
I'm halfway there
With nothing to spare
I'm trying so hard but getting nowhere
I'm trying to sleep but keep thinking instead
Of what I would be doing at home in bed
It's 11 o'clock and I'm finally there.
People just stopping to stand and stare
Across the road a baby just cried
I've got nowhere decent really to hide.
I'm drinking coffee all the time
Instead of getting mixed up in all sorts of crime
My friends have gone, gone back home
They surrendered over the phone.
I think it's time I had a rest
To go back home, the place I love best.

Michael Leslie (13)
The Heath Specialist Technology College

Yesterday, Today And Tomorrow

Yesterday
Yesterday has gone,
It has passed away.
Whatever you did yesterday,
You cannot change.
It can be sad and gloomy,
Or happy and cheerful,
You decide.

Today
Today's here,
Enjoy it while you can.
It will soon be yesterday,
Whatever you do today,
Will soon be in the past.
So try not to make
Too many bad memories.

Tomorrow
Tomorrow is coming
But . . .
Never arrives
Think about what you will do tomorrow
Plan for the future
Not the past.

Laura Merry (14)
The Heath Specialist Technology College

Racer

Tyres burning on the track.
All fixed up and ready to drive,
Speed!
Speed!
Speed!
Engine's roaring like a beast.
Driver pumped and ready to race.
Adrenaline!
Adrenaline!
Adrenaline!
Paintwork shining in the sun.
Windows gleaming and looking good.
Ready!
Ready!
Ready!
Foot on the pedal.
Hand on the gearstick.
Go!
Go!
Go!

Myles McKeever (12)
The Heath Specialist Technology College

The Octopus

An octopus is multicoloured
It is winter
In the sea
He is rainy
A deep skin
A small hat stand
A huge blockbuster
A lovely octopus dinner.

Adam Ludgate (12)
The Heath Specialist Technology College

The Spooky Forest

Deeper
Deeper into the forest
Squeaking
Mumbling
    Louder
        Louder
            Louder
                Louder
Roar!
The beast
He said, 'Come in.'
I didn't want to,
He made me
I screamed
    Help
        Help
            Help
                Help
He stretched
He got me,
I fell.
The beast got me
I
Punched
I
kicked
He'd got me for good
There was nothing,
Nothing I could do.

Scott Hatton (11)
The Heath Specialist Technology College

Liverpool Vs Chelsea

And it is off
Gerrard to Heskey
Heskey to Owen
    Running
        Running
            Running

With the ball
And
He
Shoots
He
Scores!
Cheering
Cheering
Cheering
Cheering is going on
And it's off again
Jimmy
Runs
Jimmy
Shoots
Jerzy
    Unexpectedly
        Saves
            The
                Day

One nil to Liverpool
Jerzy saved the day.

John Hatton (11)
The Heath Specialist Technology College

The Dreaded Visit

Broom!
The car started.
Sweat running down my face,
Blood pouring from my knee.
Swerving round the corners,
The seatbelt can't last and suddenly . . .
Crash!
I wake up,
White walls surrounding me.
Men in masks,
Breathing and leaning over me.
A sharp pain and a yell
It was over, at last.
There'd be scars
There'd be pain
But I'd never forget
Don't drink and drive.

Ashley Jacobs (11)
The Heath Specialist Technology College

Pilot Of A Plane

A pilot is blue
    He is the autumn
In a cockpit
    He is sundown
A pilot is a uniform
    A model plane
An airline's programme
    A pilot is a bald eagle!

Adam Jones (13)
The Heath Specialist Technology College

Yesterday Was . . .

Yesterday was cold and wet
Yesterday was happy and helpful
Yesterday was love and lonely
Yesterday

Today is freezing and frozen
Today is sunny and sad
Today is dark and frightening
Today

Tomorrow will be laughter and fun
Tomorrow will be ice and cheering
Tomorrow will be dry and clearer
Tomorrow

Cold, laughter
Wet, sadness
Happy, ice
Helpful, cheering
Love, funny
Lonely, frightening
Frozen, laughter
Dry, sunny.

Carl Riley (12)
The Heath Specialist Technology College

Time . . .

Yesterday was cold and gloomy,
Yesterday was hot and sunny,
Yesterday was dark and lonely,
Yesterday.
Today is joyful and great,
Today is timeless and wicked,
Today is Hell and Heaven,
Today.
Tomorrow will be evil and miserable,
Tomorrow will be dreamy and wonderful,
Tomorrow will be lovely and gorgeous,
Tomorrow.

Yesterday was dark and lonely,
Today was timeless and wicked,
Tomorrow will be dreamy and wonderful
Time is days
Days are time
Time is deep
Deep like my heart.

Jamie Garbutt (12)
The Heath Specialist Technology College

Yesterday Was . . .

Yesterday was dark and frightening
Yesterday was sad and lonely
Yesterday was down and cold
Yesterday

Today is light and happy
Today is exciting and sunny
Today is lovely and warm
Today

Tomorrow will be dull and scary
Tomorrow will be depressing and boring
Tomorrow will be rainy and wet
Tomorrow.

Abi Colclough (12)
The Heath Specialist Technology College

A Football Poem

It was Liverpool Vs Arsenal
At midday
The match had only one minute left
The score was 0-0
And Liverpool were on the break
It was 3 players running towards the Arsenal defence
Kewell, Baros and Owen
The defence was closing in
But Baros passed to Owen,
Owen passed to Kewell
And Kewell finished it off
1-0 in the final 10 seconds
And Liverpool had won the match.

Jack Cardus (12)
The Heath Specialist Technology College

Yesterday Was . . .

Yesterday was cold and wet
Yesterday was sad and gloomy
Yesterday was dark and frightening
Yesterday

Today is happiness and fun
Today is smiles and cheering
Today is laughter and shouting
Today

Tomorrow will be joyful and cold
Tomorrow will be dark and smiles
Tomorrow will be smiling and tears
Tomorrow

Today is frightening and sun
Today is boring and happy
Today

Yesterday is weariness and cheering
Yesterday was good and bad
Yesterday was . . .

Andrew Woodside (12)
The Heath Specialist Technology College

Yesterday Was . . .

Yesterday was cold and sunny
Yesterday was happy and joyful
Yesterday was good and bright
Yesterday.

Today is chilly and windy
Today is fun and shouting
Today is great and cheering
Today.

Tomorrow is sad and frightening
Tomorrow is rainy and wet
Tomorrow is colourful and slow
Tomorrow.

Sad, coldness
Frightening, sun
Raining, happily
Wet, joyfully
Colourful, goodness
Slow, brightness.

Paul Dempsey (13)
The Heath Specialist Technology College

Yesterday Was . . .

Yesterday was cold and gloomy
Yesterday was wet and boring
Yesterday was sad and lonely
Yesterday.

Today is laughter and fun
Today is love and smiling
Today is sunshine and heat
Today.

Tomorrow will be joyful and great
Tomorrow will be happy and dreamy
Tomorrow will be warm and hot
Tomorrow.

Sunshine, smiles
Lovely, happiness
Laughing, warmth
Sad, heat
Wet, joyful
Cold, fun
Hot, loneliness
Gloomy, heat
Boring, great.

Steph Jenkinson (12)
The Heath Specialist Technology College

Yesterday Was . . .

Yesterday was cold and gloomy
Yesterday was hateful and rainy
Yesterday was light and cloudy
Yesterday.

Today is boring and dark
Today is fun and happy
Today is sad and dull
Today.

Tomorrow will be hot and sunny
Tomorrow will be freezing and windy
Tomorrow will be horrible and delightful
Tomorrow.

Cold, hot
Hateful, fun
Gloomy, delightful
Cloudy, wind
Dark, horribleness
Happy, dullness.

Michael Buckley (12)
The Heath Specialist Technology College

Happy Holiday

In the sea,
On the sand,
In the room,
On the bed.

The sun is out,
And so are we,
First it was warm,
But now it's hot,
Hot,
Hot!

Sunbathing,
Playing
It's all that we do,
Except for when the ice cream's here,
We all run and shout.

Chloe Anwyll (11)
The Heath Specialist Technology College

Flowers

Flowers are bright
They are the summer
They are warm
They fill the garden
They make the sunshine bright
Bright like cheerful clothing
Full like a school
Colourful like a young child's TV
Different colours like a salad.

Sarah Worrall (12)
The Heath Specialist Technology College

The Flip

Getting changed
Very nervous
Can she do it?
Practising
Very nervous
Will it work?
Waiting for her turn
Very nervous
Will they like it?
Her chance is nearly here
Very nervous
What will happen?
Here is her chance
More nervous than ever
Will she get hurt?

OK.
Go..
Going fine
Not too nervous
Here it comes
Take a runner
Bend your knees
Build your confidence
Think positive
Don't look down and . . .
Yes, yes, yes!
She has done it
It did work
They did like it
It was great
And she is fine.

Lisa Merriman (11)
The Heath Specialist Technology College

Roller Coaster

Got to get on
Rushing for the line
Get into the queue
Waiting forever
Heart beating
Check height, can get on

Jump into the seat
Pull down barrier
Man checks everyone is safe
Man disappears
Ready to go.

Big voice counts, '1, 2, 3'
Goes silent
Whoosh!
We fly up into the air
A drop quickly back down
Up again
Everyone is screaming.

Comes down calmly
Everyone is smiling
Jump out of seat.

Rushes again to line.

Emma Platt (11)
The Heath Specialist Technology College

At The Beach

Running
Running
Across the golden sand
No one there to bother you
Except for your mum and dad.
The sea glistening
Your heart racing
You
Drop
To
The
Floor
The ice-cold touch
Of the splashing sea
Running through your toes.

Rebecca Travis (11)
The Heath Specialist Technology College

The Beach

The beach wasn't fun
It was meant to be
But it wasn't.

The sheer thrill of volleyball
With the waves crashing against my ankles
Like white horses running.
A picnic with sand sandwiches
And salt-tasting water.

The lifeguard didn't see her,
Didn't see her,
Didn't see her,
It was such a sad end.

I will never forget
The day at the beach.

Leah Connolly (11)
The Heath Specialist Technology College

A Haunted House

Cold!
    Damp!
        Dark!
            Alone!
Terror haunts me behind

Slowly
I venture up the path
The gravel grinding
With my shoe soles.

Daringly
Terribly
Scared
I opened the door.

Large
Twisted
Towering
Figures
Peer down on me
Like an ant

There stood a
Frail
Stubborn
Figure.

And then . . .

Craig Smith (12)
The Heath Specialist Technology College

Detention

Our English teacher said,
'Write a poem.'
I was stuck for ideas
I usually could write it easily
But what I said was,
'Miss, I can't do it.'
She said, 'There's no such word as *can't.'*
I was stuck, I was really
Stuck.
'Miss, I cannot do it.'
'Detention for cheek
And answering a teacher back.
Remember, there's always
A 'can' in 'can't'.'
I felt dark and evil
What was detention?
Did it send you
To a lifetime of evilness?
What's going to happen to me?
Bye life.
Bye
Bye
Bye
A pure 'A' record
Stolen by the word
'Can't'.

Amy Goldsmith (11)
The Heath Specialist Technology College

Boredom

Here I am,
At my nan's,
I'm bored already,
        Bored,
            Bored,
                Bored.

I don't know why I'm here,
But I do know I wish I wasn't,
There's nothing to do,
        Nothing,
            Nothing,
                Nothing.

There's nothing to do,
Nothing to play,
        Why?
            Why?
                Why?
    Why am I here?

Charlene Hayes (11)
The Heath Specialist Technology College

My Dog!

My dog is black
He is the summer
On my bed
Wears no clothes
He is a furry cushion
A TV advert
Chicken in gravy.

Jaycee Butterworth (13)
The Heath Specialist Technology College

The Boyfriend

I said, 'Do you hate me?'
I said, 'How d'you feel?'
I said, 'Behind the bike shed.'
I said, 'I fancy you.'

He said, 'Yeah whatever.'
He said, 'Are you real?'
He said, 'Say what?'
He said, 'Tonight at 8.'

I said, 'Do you like me?'
I said, 'Let's hold hands!'
I said, 'Come on!'
I said, 'You've really turned around!'

He said, 'Yeah OK!'
He said, 'This is great!'
He said, 'Let's go out!'
He said, 'Maybe Sunday.'

Gemma Collins (12)
The Heath Specialist Technology College

Army Man

An army man is green,
He is the green spring leaves,
He is a jungle,
He fires his gun like lightning,
An army man is camouflaged,
He is a tall grandfather clock,
He is a warm film,
He eats anything.

Connor Ashley (13)
The Heath Specialist Technology College

Asylum?

I left the worst place ever
I left the blood
        the bombs
I left my family
        my friends
        my home

To come to a peaceful
        a pleasant
        a calm place
To come to a helpful
        a beautiful
        an indescribable place

That's what I thought

I've come to a cell
        a dungeon
        a small place
I've come to a living hell
        more violence
        more hate

Not what I thought and I want to go home.

Melissa Felton (14)
The Heath Specialist Technology College

Asylum?

I wanted to leave so bad
Kinda wish I hadn't now
I wanted to leave
Blood
Violence
Abuse
Hell
Even *death*
What's better now?
A cell with no freedom?
I wanted to leave my family Hell
I wanted to leave my abusive mess
Or so I thought
Now I'm awakening in a cell
The light drifting through the window!

My childhood dream shattered
All I could do was remember the good times,
As there are none now
Just Hell
Hell
Hell!

Nikita Langley (13)
The Heath Specialist Technology College

Asylum?

I left behind
my life
death
Hell
I am
running
running
away

I am here
because
the countryside's
quiet
compared to home
this is Heaven
to
me

The cell
is
lifeless
dull
should I have come?
I
don't
think
so!

Jack Burbidge (13)
The Heath Specialist Technology College

Asylum?

I didn't feel safe
Wanted to go
I was scared
        Cheshire?
    Yes Cheshire!
Green grass,
Colourful flowers,
        No bombs!
            No killing!
                No fighting
Waking me up in the morning.
Get away from
        Hell,
            Horror,
                Home.
I left home
    Never stayed
I left
Came to Cheshire
    Happy,
        Freedom,
            Safe,
It's all over,
Went straight in a cell.

Cold,
    Lonely,
        Frightened
It was horrible
    Square room,
        Hard bed,
            Damp walls,
                Dirty floor.

What else do I need?
    Hell?
        Left Hell?
            Even more Hell?

Lee-arna Worth (13)
The Heath Specialist Technology College

Asylum?

I just had to leave
Get away from that terrible place
The place many years ago I grew up.
The place I used to enjoy being
Hell
That's what it is now
Hell

Thought it would be best to leave
Or so I thought
I thought Cheshire to be quiet
To be peaceful
To be calm

I thought wrong!
I'm locked up in a cell
Dirty
Smelly
Damp
Dark
Small
What was I thinking?
No freedom
Stuck inside a small hideous place.

I would rather go back to the living hell
At least I would have freedom
There were people to talk to
Lonely
So lonely
I feel so alone!

Stephanie Birchall (13)
The Heath Specialist Technology College

Asylum

Frightened by death
Frightened by gunshots
Frightened
I'm free from it
So I thought!
I've traded one Hell
For another
My fear remains
But it's
Growing
Growing
More
More frightened I've become
Every day
Every hair
Every second I wait
My fear growing
The questions
Will I stay?
Sitting
Cold
In a cell
Am I a prisoner?
Suddenly it came to me
The question
Will I ever be free?
Free
Freedom
Freedom from Hell
Both Hells.

Adam Craig (13)
The Heath Specialist Technology College

Hell Again

I left,
Blood,
Pain,
Bombs,
Gunfire,
Screams!
Crying,
So much violence,
Hell,
Death!

I came here for . . .
Peace,
Friends,
Health,
Happiness,
Safety,
Heaven,
Life!

I'm treated like . . .
Vermin,
Dirt.
I'm afraid,
Lonely,
Locked away,
Cramped and smelly,
In Hell again.

I wish I could go home,
No!
I wish I could die,
Leave everything,
Be free,
Free!

Sarah Canavan (13)
The Heath Specialist Technology College

Asylum?

I left everything behind
Well that's what I thought,
I thought I was leaving away
The pain,
The suffering,
The blood and death,
But I was wrong!
Every day, woken up by explosions
Every night, rocked to sleep by gunshots
I left it all behind
I fled to Cheshire.
Where sunshine wasn't full with smoke from bombs
I thought I would be treated better
I was misled
Instead I was put in a camp cell
It felt like I was put in a jail for something I hadn't done
Some of us prefer
The explosions,
The gunshots,
The bombs.
It was home,
Home sweet home.

Louise Rusling (13)
The Heath Specialist Technology College

I Need To Escape

I needed to get away from
The horror,
The terror.
I was surrounded by Taliban.
Heavy fighting all around,
I was so afraid,
A land mine could go off,
And explode the ground,
I left,
I fled from
People killing,
People dying,
I have lost my family,
Because of the
Gunshots,
Blood spilt all around,
Why can't it stop?

Cheshire seemed peaceful,
No fighting around,
No bombs in the ground,
I should be safe,
I think I will,
Or so I thought!

I got took
To Hell,
To a prison,
To a dark, damp, cold place,
My voice echoes,
In the lonely room,
No one to hear my pleas.

What have I done wrong?
Or is the world just a hateful place,
I need to escape,
I'd rather go home,
I need to escape,
From this hellhole,
I've got to get away,
Where I can be
Free as a bird
And as happy as can be.

But for now,
I am trapped,
In a place,
Made of hate,
I need to escape,
I just need to escape.

Charlotte Murison (13)
The Heath Specialist Technology College

The Doctor's

Waiting . . .
Waiting . . .
Waiting . . .
I think am I going mad?

There was the next person going and waiting.

There was lots of noise,
Drilling in my head
When everyone moved
It was like screeching,
They missed me out,
Someone was screaming.

And then there was chaos
People were screaming
People were crying.

Thomas Duncalf (12)
The Heath Specialist Technology College

Asylum Hell

I couldn't take it anymore,
Gunshots,
Explosions,
People dying,
It was all too much,
So I left,
I left everything,
I left Hell,
I left murder,
Or so I thought.

Cheshire seemed quiet,
Seemed caring,
Seemed safe,
Oh how wrong I was.

Danger was what I escaped from,
Was what I was scared of,
Was what I came to.

The jail-like place I know must call home,
Is worse than what I escaped from,
It's cold,
Lonely,
Empty,
And that's not the half of it.

I am treated like a murderer,
Though I have done nothing wrong.
Why did I choose to come here?
I would rather die than face these cold-hearted people.

Jennifer Rhodes (13)
The Heath Specialist Technology College

Asylum Poem

Frightened I was
Frightened of death
My life back there was Hell
That's why I'm here
The gunshots
The horror
That's why I'm here
The small cell was horrible
It was very cramped
But I'm safe here
Safe from that hell hole
Safe from death!
Now I am a prisoner
Without my family
Mum
Dad
My sister
All of them gone
But at least
They're in a better place
A better place
Without me.

Stefan Evans (13)
The Heath Specialist Technology College

Asylum?

I had left it all
At least that's what I thought
The awakening gunshots
The midday landmines
It's all gone
Gone for good
I left blood
I left death
I even left Hell
And where was I put?
I was put in a cell
They threw me in
They locked the door
Was this the end of me?
Well, that's what I thought.

Louise Hignett (13)
The Heath Specialist Technology College

Love

Love is red
It is all year round
In a heart
It is warm
Love is silk
A small stepladder
In every programme
A red apple that could turn black!

Tanya McDonnell (13)
The Heath Specialist Technology College

Asylum?

I left,
I left the violence,
I left my possessions,
I left my so called home.

    I entered a totally different country.

Now I am a cell,
Now I am in Hell.

    I wish I never came
But I had to.

        I miss my
            Mum
                Dad
                    And family

I left
So I thought
I left.

Alison Fletcher (14)
The Heath Specialist Technology College

Asylum Poem

A sudden silent
Waiting, patiently
Waiting
    Waiting
        Waiting
For the sound of the gunshot.

The loud gunshot
Leaves me alarmed
Waiting anxiously
For it to appear again

I hear the officer's keys rattle
I hear the cell doors
Opening for breakfast.

I am starving, hungry
Is my door open?
I don't think so
Or so I thought . . .

Victoria Routledge (13)
The Heath Specialist Technology College

Asylum?

Goodbye fear
Goodbye death
Goodbye Hell
Hello Heaven
Hello freedom
Hello safety
Or so I thought
I entered with hopes and expectations
But I entered a cell, with 10 other people.
I had done nothing wrong
Bang!
Bang!
Bang!
As my father went down
I fled as fast as I could
To a country so safe
Caring, heart-warming
Country, Cheshire
Here I am now; cold
Scared
Behind jail bars!

Faye Carmichael (13)
The Heath Specialist Technology College

Walk Down Memory Lane

If you hear the crunch of frosty grass,
If you see the green of a long sprouted blade,
Just stop and take it in.

When the cool wind blows through your hair,
Or the cold, wet rain dampens your soft skin,
Or maybe you feel the bright, intense rays
Of the dazzling sun,
Just spare a moment, memorise the feeling.

If you hear the trickle of water,
Or maybe feel the cold sensation it leaves you,
Absorb the feelings and the vibes it sends out.

The next time the relaxing chirp of a bird,
Or the scuttle of a tired badger,
Maybe even the ear-piercing song of a dolphin,
Please, for me, spend a moment and take it in.

Maybe you are so lucky as to come upon a ruin,
Feel, is it smooth or rough?
How does it smell, sweet or aged?
Please observe carefully.

Cora Carlin (11)
The Heath Specialist Technology College

Arguing With Your Mum

You said I could have credit on my phone
You said you would be good
You said I could have a fiver for pocket money
You said you would do your room.

I said you were nasty
I said you were bad
I said you were horrible
I said you were cheeky.

You said I could have a PlayStation 2
You said you would be nice to your brother
You said I could go to my mates
You said you would keep quiet.

I said you are shady
I said you shouldn't have been naughty
I said you don't let me do anything
I said you're grounded.

Chelsea Garbutt (11)
The Heath Specialist Technology College

A Band

A band is bright,
And fills up summer
In the studio.
They are always sunny,
And wearing their best,
Their hair is even their own style.
They are our porcelain dolls,
Our pop idols,
And our little pieces of chocolate!

Danielle Lewis (12)
The Heath Specialist Technology College

Gone

She looked up at the starry night
The wind pushed her on
She ran and wished she was gone
She looked up at the starry night
Nothing was as it seemed
The wind never stopped
The sky would not tell
About the girl who was never more.
Nobody missed her
Nobody cared
The only thing that saw her was the air.
She was gone,
It managed to whistle
Into a dark, eerie gloom
She was at home you see,
After the wish she was not . . .
Alone.

Rebecca Allen (11)
The Heath Specialist Technology College

Mother And Daughter

You said I could have my phone credit
You said you'd be good
You said I could have it today
You said you won't be cheeky

I said you were boring
I said you were cheeky
I said you were horrible
I said you were cheeky

You said I was horrible
You said I was boring
You said I was cheeky
You said I was horrible

I said please
I said no
I said I am sorry
I said so

You said it's tough
You said so
You said I don't care
You said neither do I.

Now we aren't talking
Our friendship's gone
Gone
Gone
Never to come back.

Zara Pavey (11)
The Heath Specialist Technology College

The Worst Day Out Ever

As I waited,
In the waiting room
With bare white walls
Waiting for the dentist to call my name
Will it be soon?
I hope not!
'I hope so,' Mum replied
As she was falling asleep,
'Next!' shouted
            The
                Dentist.

Oh no, it's me
As I sat in the cold chair
Waiting
Still waiting
Here he comes, 'Open wide.'
Slowly opening my mouth
He puts the cold drill into my mouth
All I can hear is the buzzing

I want my mum
I want to go home
    Please
    Please.

Jade Stoddart (11)
The Heath Specialist Technology College

Looking In The Mirror

Looking in the mirror
Staring at a figure,
Spoiling happiness,
By looking in the mirror.

We have no control over it now,
It is our problem,
With hurt and anger,
And . . . why me?

Looking in the mirror

Afraid to see me,
Afraid to see me,
I feel deformed,
I feel hurt,
I feel lonely,
Because . . . of looking in the mirror.

Nicola Merry (13)
The Heath Specialist Technology College

The Cat

They should have checked on their cat.
The cat walked proudly in the middle of the night,
It went to the park where there was no one in sight.
It chased a bird up a tree,
He got stuck and no one could see.

In the morning his bright blue eyes were lifeless,
His tail dropped, it was motionless,
He started crying like a waterfall,
Then a passer-by came, called by his purring call.

The boy looked up to see the cat in the tree,
The boy knew he was saying, 'Help me, help me.'
The boy climbed up the trunk like a monkey,
Brought the cat down and let him free.

The cat dragged himself home tiredly,
Where he saw his worried family.
They gave him a cuddle like they were insane
And they told him never to run off again.

Robert Ryan (11)
The Heath Specialist Technology College

Conversation

I said, 'Yes.'
She said, 'Fine.'
I said, 'Never.'
She said, 'Whatever.'

I screamed, 'Go away!'
She screamed, 'Why don't you?'
I screamed, 'You're not getting your own way.'
She screamed, 'I don't intend to.'

I shouted, 'Leave me alone.'
She shouted, 'I'm going home.'
I shouted, 'Fine by me.'
She shouted, 'Don't call me.'

She yelled, 'Don't bother following me.'
I yelled, 'I'm off for my tea.'
She yelled, 'Hope you choke.'
I yelled, 'Not a hope.'

Jenny Jones (12)
The Heath Specialist Technology College

An Argument That I Will Never Forget . . .

Mum said, 'We're going to the beach.'
I said, 'That sounds great.'
Mum shouted, 'Hurry up.'
I replied, 'Why? We won't be late.'

Mum shouted, 'Get into the car.'
I said, 'Yes, I'm coming now.'
Mum screamed, 'Don't give me cheek.'
I said, 'Shut up, you nasty cow.'

Mum said, 'I'm not going!'
I said, 'That's not fair, why?'
Mum said, 'Not until you apologise!'
I said, 'Sorry,' and pretended to cry.

Mum said, 'Let's get going.'
I replied, 'OK!'
Mum said, 'I hope you enjoy it.'
I replied, 'We'll have a really great day!'

Michaela Horner (12)
The Heath Specialist Technology College

Youth And Old Age

Age and youth,
Cannot live together,
Age is needing help,
Youth is being independent,
Age like a mouse, curled up to sleep,
Youth like a cat, waiting for a chance,
Age is mithered, seeking a memory,
Youth is sharp, needing to know,
Age is knowledge,
Youth is learning,
Age is ill and weak,
Youth is fit and strong,
Age is cautious,
Youth is a danger,
Age I need your wisdom,
Youth I need your carefree life.

Lucy Hancock (12)
The Heath Specialist Technology College

Ivory Tower

In a place of torment and perpetual fear,
And a world of cold hearts not willing to hear,
Flows anger and confusion from those she held dear.
It is somewhere she's trapped in,
Though freedom is near.

Their monotone statements follow where she roams
And hurt filled with laughter is brought on and droned.
But the princess in the tower knows her way out,
Understands who her friends are
Of them there's no doubt.

So she moves through the darkness and into the light
And the others can't follow though untied to the night.
For all their intentions they've damaged her start.
Now the princess escapes
And follows her heart . . .

Beth Birmingham (18)
Widnes & Runcorn VI Form College

The Living Dead

Two weeks ago, I died
with medical smells and blinding whites -
the doctor, my artist, smearing red paint
on a dry canvas.

Two weeks ago, I died
a beautiful death with smiles and tears,
with hands on backs and polite goodbyes -
'She was such a lovely girl'.

Two weeks ago, he cried -
another comfort missed and gone.
No cleaner of pots or womanly touch -
see why I wanted to go?

Two weeks ago, I died -
stomach bulged with a useless weight.
He'll cry for the child I couldn't provide,
then complain about the prices.

Two weeks ago, I died,
but not before my child had rot inside.
Taking the blade and with a clean suicide,
I live here dead with my pain still alive.

Hayley Bruffell (17)
Widnes & Runcorn VI Form College

Can You Hear Them?

Listen . . . can you hear them, the lonely?
Wandering in the shadow of death, they elude us no more.
Living in our lies, cover them in foil so they shall not toil . . .

Awake no longer, though never truly asleep,
We hide our faces within a shallow deep . . .
Can you hear them?
Cold and unforgiven, whispering to the moon cursed by stars . . .
No longer locked behind the shackles of iron bars!

Given nothing, they became a twisted fantasy . . .
We cut all ties, connections and bonds, though we make them
drink from rancid ponds . . .
We revel in their pain like some sick ecstasy!
Can you hear them?

As they lie on ground, embraced by the cold and the frost . . .
we will never truly find them . . .
Are they forever lost?

Adam Woodward (16)
Widnes & Runcorn VI Form College

I Won't Forget You!

I will never forget like the
Sun does,
When it rises up in the sky
For a brand new day.
It forgets all the problems of the world
And carries on shining
In that bright, beaming way.

I will never forget the way the
Moon does,
When it lights up the night
With the stars.
Its only concern is the tide - rolling in.
The moon doesn't hold feelings
Like ours.

I will always remember the way that the
Rain does,
When it rains, then rises, then rains.
It touches us, then it disappears,
(Only to touch us again!)
It is there all of the time.
(Like the blood - through our veins.)

I will never forget like the
Sun does,
Like the moon and the stars in the sky.
I will remember,
Just like the raindrops
As they fall.
(Like tears - from my eyes.)

Ellen Adshead (17)
Widnes & Runcorn VI Form College